Content

About the author

Elisa is a professional language teacher and a language enthusiast. She teaches Italian, German, English, Spanish, Russian, French, Dutch, Catalan, Portuguese, Greek, Hindi, Arabic and Esperanto (at different levels) to both children and adults. She is specialised in multilingual teaching (where students learn multiple languages at the same time, within one course) and is a certified language examiner for English, French, German, Italian, Russian and Spanish. She has taught and lived in several countries (including the UK, Russia, Germany, Spain, Switzerland and Italy), and holds two BAs in Translation and Interpreting, as well as MAs in International Communication and Didactics respectively.

She regularly gives presentations on language learning, multilingual teaching and learning and intercultural communication, and teaches workshops in which participants start speaking one or more languages from the very first moment and have their first conversation after just a few minutes. She is also a multilingual mentor and a language coach and can help you speed up your language learning.

Introduction

I have met so many people who want to learn languages but they feel demotivated because: a) they don't think they are good at languages, b) they studied in the past but didn't achieve the results they were hoping for, c) they can't establish a successful study routine, d) they didn't enjoy learning languages at school, or e) they have little free time and are waiting for the right moment to start learning (which normally never comes).

I have also met many people who are interested in learning more than one language, but they don't dare to get started because: a) they aren't sure whether it's a good idea to study these languages together, b) they really would like to learn them but are discouraged from doing so at the same time, c) they are afraid to mix languages up, or d) they have tried to learn more than one language at the same time but either felt it overwhelming or mixed the languages up.

I have written this book precisely for those people. To all of you, I would like to say that anyone can learn languages. What's more, anyone can learn more than one language at the same time without mixing them up. It IS possible because hundreds of students have already done it and not only does it work, but there are clear advantages in doing so. It's just a matter of method.

I love languages; I have studied 24 languages myself and brought 13 of them to a teaching level. However, I was not born multilingual. In fact, I learnt all of my languages (apart from French and my native language) from the age of 20 onwards. At the beginning, I didn't know how to learn languages in an efficient way, so I tried out many different methods. I also studied translation and interpreting, and I have an MA in Didactics. I have been teaching for 20 years now and have experimented with different strategies which have helped me understand what works not only for me but for everyone else! I love helping people become fluent, overcome their fears, and reach their goals. One of the best rewards is to see my students happy when they see the amazing progress they are making and when I know that they feel more and more confident in the language(s) they want to learn.

My passion and interest in languages led me to start learning multiple languages at the same time many years ago. When I noticed that other people shared my interest and enthusiasm, I started offering multilingual lessons and writing multilingual learning material. Since then I have regularly given talks on multilingual learning and practical workshops where my students start speaking multiple languages after just a few minutes.

In this book, you will find a detailed description of my multilingual method, a method that anyone can follow to learn multiple languages at the same time without mixing them up. It involves easy steps and fun activities, many efficient learning strategies for learning any language (as well as one at a time too), and examples of efficient study routine, tools and strategies to keep you motivated. Even though it may seem like a challenge, learning more than one language at the same time is not only possible but also speeds up your learning process, and even just five minutes a day, provided you use them efficiently (a methodology widely explained throughout this book), are enough to help you see amazing results and become more confident in your language(s). So don't wait any longer, get started now!

Part 1

Why learn more than one language at the same time?

The first and most important reason why you 'should' learn more than one language at the same time is that YOU are interested in more than one language. And what YOU really want is what matters. Why wait for years before starting to do what you are CURRENTLY interested in?

If you are thinking about learning more than one language at the same time, it means that you are <u>already</u> interested in more than one language.

Of course, the reason for learning more than one language varies from person to person, but it may have something to do with a partner who speaks a different language, a country you would like to live in or visit, a job for which a certain language could be important, good friends from another country or just curiosity about other languages and cultures. It could also be that a certain language speaks to your heart or because you just love the way certain languages sound.

Whatever the reason, if it's important to you, why wait for years before starting to do what you want to do today?

People who say that you should only learn one language at a time normally mean that you should first reach an advanced level before you start learning a new one. Reaching an advanced level in a language normally takes at least one or two years, if not longer. If you've got a good reason to learn a language now (for example, you really need a language certificate in order to emigrate, you are going to travel this year and you want to be able to speak with locals, or your partner or kids speak languages you don't understand), why wait?!

Let's clarify an obvious point: of course, if YOU are interested in just one language, there is no reason why you should study more than one language (unless you have to). But, in my experience, many people are interested in multiple languages.

In my case, I started to learn multiple languages at the same time because I love making sense of what I don't understand, I enjoy challenges and, above all, I love connecting with people and understanding other cultures and mentalities!

The reasons vary from person to person, but if you are genuinely interested in lots of languages, then why not give it a go? I always say that learning multiple languages must come from a place of interest and motivation, but **everyone should know that it IS possible and that it has many advantages**.

Is it possible to learn more than one language at the same time?

If you'd like to do it but are hesitant because some people say it's crazy... honestly, why let yourself be influenced by what other people think isn't possible? **It IS possible** because I have done it myself and I have helped hundreds of people to learn more than one language without mixing them up.

In my experience, when people say that something isn't possible, it's usually because they haven't used the right method! (And in some cases, they haven't tried to do it at all!)

A quote I like states: "Everyone said it was impossible. Then one day, someone, who was unaware of how challenging it was, just came along and did it".

Do what YOU love, believe in yourself and follow your dreams.

If you have tried to learn multiple languages at the same time and it didn't work out, I am 100% convinced that it was due to the method used – not your ability! With the right method, anyone can learn!

Learning several languages at the same time is possible: <u>everyone is able to learn different things at the same time</u>. We do it every day. We learn and carry out different tasks the whole day, every day. No kid will ever say: "Sorry Mum, I'm learning how to brush my teeth, how can I also learn how to put my toys back into the box after playing?!" In the same way, no adult would say at work: "Sorry, I'm learning how to do X so I can't learn how to do Y."

Now that it's clear that we constantly learn several things at the same time (at the same time does not mean at the exact same moment), let's address the two biggest concerns regarding this topic, which are actually two of the MAIN reasons why learning several languages at the same time is a great idea.

The two main concerns: mixing languages up and language learning speed

The biggest concerns when it comes to learning multiple languages at the same time relate to the fear or experience of **mixing languages up** and **language learning speed**, as many people think it takes much longer to learn more than one language at the same time and prefer to concentrate on one language.

Many people think that if you study multiple languages at the same time, you will mix languages up. In fact, contrary to what people generally think, **learning languages at the same time HELPS you AVOID mixing up languages**. To better explain this point, let's have a look at the reasons <u>why people mix languages up</u>. I spoke to hundreds of people to understand the causes and I have seen recurring patterns. One or more of these points are always true:

1) They speak (or learn) one language much more often than the other(s), so the brain goes back to the more frequently-used (or learnt) language.

2) They rarely speak these languages.

3) They know one of the languages very well but the other(s) not as well in comparison, and they don't practise the newer one(s).

4) They are not used to switching between languages.

5) The language features of one or more languages are not clear yet. Language features are the recurrent differences between two similar languages or special characteristics of a given language. If we are aware of the way two similar languages change respect to each other (e.g. between Spanish and Italian: 'a**ctor**' v 'a**ttore**', 'dire**ctor**' v 'dire**ttore**'; 'pens**ar**' v 'pens**are**', 'dorm**ir**' v 'dorm**ire**', '**ci**erto' v '**c**erto', etc.), OR their recurrent patterns or distinctive markers (e.g. Portuguese: many words end in '**ão**' like 'cora**ção**', 'ent**ão**' and 'n**ão**', and this does not happen in other Romance languages like French, Spanish,

Italian, Catalan, etc.).

You may find yourself in one or more of these categories, but you should know that it does not have to be this way. I have been in the same situation and many others experience a similar type of frustration when they put time and effort into learning and get little in the way of results. And above all, you may end up feeling inadequate when you try to speak a language that you either learnt in the past or are learning now. In this book, I will describe the method and language learning strategies I have used for many years and have taught to hundreds of students so that they too can successfully learn all the languages they want to learn, without mixing them up.

My first and very simple piece of advice for those who want to stop mixing languages up is to **get enough speaking practice in their target languages**.

It also helps if you **focus on the differences between languages and on their language features**. In doing so, your brain will be aware of the differences and this will affect the way you speak. This last point can really speed up your learning process and enhance your ability to switch between languages. Regardless, as long as you practise your languages enough, you will make progress.

You can identify the language features by yourself and train your speaking skills through other productive activities, such as writing, or you could have someone else help you. Multilingual lessons are very effective because your multilingual teacher knows all the languages you want to learn and can help you a) clarify language features and b) switch from one language to another, which significantly helps to keep languages separate in the brain. It normally only takes two or three multilingual lessons before my students almost stop mixing up their languages altogether – and they start speaking all the languages from day one.

Learning languages together is useful because you will get used to switching from one to the other from the very beginning. It's much easier to form a new habit than change an old one, so the earlier you learn to distinguish between two languages you want to learn, the better. The second reason why learning languages together is useful is that you will learn them more quickly. This takes us to the second concern people have regarding multilingual learning: the learning pace. Many people think that learning multiple languages will slow down your learning. In fact, **learning languages at the same time will <u>speed up</u> your learning process**.

A big advantage of learning multiple languages together is that the time you spend learning languages is NOT proportional to the number of languages you learn. To understand this, first we'll look at learning **similar languages** at the same time and then consider languages which belong to **different language families**.

When you learn two (or more) **similar languages** at the same time, there are obvious advantages in terms of **grammar**. Once you have understood a certain grammar point in one language, it takes considerably less time to understand and use the same (or similar) grammar point in another language. For example, when I teach Italian, Spanish and French in the same lesson, it normally takes 10 to 15 minutes for my students to understand and use the past tense in Italian, so logic would suggest that to learn the rules for the three languages would take 45 minutes. In reality, students on my multilingual courses (online and in person) usually need 10 to 15 minutes for the first language, but it takes them only a couple of minutes more to use similar forms in the other two. That's about 20-25 minutes v the ~45 minutes it would otherwise take.

When it comes to **vocabulary**, it takes even less time and effort to understand and use similar words. You don't have to learn everything from scratch with each language, you just have to <u>learn the differences</u>.

Of course, you can also do this AFTER having learnt a language. But, once you're <u>fluent</u> in a language, you don't normally think about grammar rules anymore. So, when you start learning a new similar language, you have to revise that same (or similar) rule again, wasting precious time. When you learn similar languages at the same time, you don't have to <u>remember</u> the rule because you have just heard it. Besides, because grammar rules and/or words are similar, for your brain it's as if you are revising them when you are actually hearing them for the first time.

So, if you are genuinely interested in multiple languages but are worried that learning them at the same time will slow down your learning pace, you'll be please to know that it's exactly the opposite. The time you spend learning similar languages is in no way proportional to the number of languages you learn. To give you an example with numbers, if it takes you one year to become fluent in one language, learning multiple similar languages at the same time means that it will take you <u>almost</u> the same amount of time to learn the others. This is because you pick up similar grammar rules almost immediately and because anything similar that you read and hear in one language helps you take your revision to the next level. It's like killing two birds with one stone!

What happens when we learn languages from **different language families**?

Even if you're looking to learning languages from different families, there are several advantages. On one hand, if you combine similar languages to one or more non-similar languages, your brain will thank you. It's like giving your brain a break without taking a rest. For example, if you study Italian and French together and then switch to German, for your brain it's as if you are carrying out a different activity and when you go back to a similar language, let's say Spanish, you will be ready to absorb new information again.

On the other hand, if you only learn languages from different families, you lose the benefit of similar vocabulary. BUT no matter the languages you want to learn, learning several languages at the same time will help you develop your language skills, and improve your general understanding of grammar and how languages work. All of this will help you pick up new bits of languages much more quickly.

Additionally, even languages which don't seem to have much in common have similarities. I have studied 24 languages and I was surprised by the way each language helped me with other languages at some point or another. Sometimes it was a word, grammar point, sound or expression which was similar in another language, and other times it was the <u>mental association</u> that a certain word provoked in my mind.

If you have already tried to learn different dances, you will know that everything you learn in one dance will help you improve the others (also if you learn them at the same time), because many of the principles behind them are similar. The same happens with languages.

There are clear advantages in learning more than one language at the same time, <u>in terms of time and efficiency</u>, but I know that the only person who can decide whether it makes sense for you...is you!

If you are <u>already</u> interested in more than one language and knowing them is important to you and to your life <u>now</u>, why wait for years before starting to do what you want to do today?

Learning multiple languages at the same time <u>is possible</u> and if you are motivated and are doing it for the right reasons, then why not do it?!

It is really just a matter of method! Anyone, with the right method, can learn one or more languages at the same time.

If other people (polyglots included) advise you against multilingual learning but you are truly interested in doing so, think about it for a second: why should other people tell you what you can and can't do? They don't know you, so they can only say what didn't work for them. Everyone is different. What's important to remember is that if someone doesn't succeed in doing something, it's due to factors linked to their life – not yours!

Once again: do what YOU love, believe in yourself and follow your dreams.

Part 2

Is multilingual learning for me?

Learning more than one language at the same is a **wonderful opportunity** for those who want to learn quickly and with the **best possible return on time investment**, as described in Part 1.

Multilingual learning is for those who don't want to mix languages up or learn a new language and **forget the previous one(s)**.

Above all, multilingual learning is a great method for those who love languages and **don't want to wait years before starting to learn the other language(s) they are interested in**.

Multilingual learning is also for those who have already faced the struggle of learning languages and **have not (yet!) obtained the results they hoped for**.

Some of you may think that you aren't 'good' at learning languages. If this sounds like you, you probably didn't enjoy learning languages at school or, if you did, you don't remember much of the language(s) anymore, especially if you haven't used them much since then.

I felt the same way for a while. I was not born bilingual but after taking a trip with my mum, I started to feel like languages meant something to me. At primary school, we had an English native speaker for a short period of time, but all I remember is that I felt terrible the whole time because I couldn't remember anything 'taught' in class.

I was very passionate about French but despite doing all of my homework, when I went to secondary school,

I realised that I knew very little and my first term was a complete disaster. French was my first foreign language and I didn't know much about language learning.

During my teens, I also tried to learn other languages on my own, such as English, Spanish and German.

The problem was that I had no method and my results were close to zero. I tried to learn by using some books – not very helpful ones I can say now that I have 20 years' experience in language learning and teaching – and by memorising words. Despite lots of effort, I only knew some words, I couldn't make sentences and I certainly couldn't speak. Languages really interested me, but I didn't know how to learn them.

Now I am even more passionate about languages. I have studied 24 languages and teach 13 of them: I love helping people reach their language goals in a quick and interactive way.

I have taught at universities and in language schools, but now I prefer to help people around the world by teaching online and through my online single-language and multilingual courses, e-books and podcasts. I also have my own website, www.speakfromdayonewithelisa.com, where plenty of information and videos about me and my method can be found.

In secondary school, despite my disastrous first-term French results, I was determined to learn the language I loved so much. I studied so much and so hard that by the end of the second term, I was the best in my French class. I still hadn't developed a real method, but I started to understand what worked. I kept studying French for years, trying out different learning strategies. I wasn't actually aware of what I was doing, I just tried anything and everything that was available to me in order to learn my beloved language: Mickey Mouse videos in French bought on a trip with my father, magazines on any topic I could find in my city (from girly magazines to psychology), anthologies with French excerpts of literary works (which I decided to read during a very boring summer when I couldn't go anywhere and instead fell in love with the 'Little Prince' by Antoine de Saint-Exupéry), etc.

I also really wanted to listen to lots of French and since we didn't have a TV antenna, I worked alongside my university studies in order to buy one (no Amazon video, YouTube or Netflix at the time, sorry).

But French wasn't my only passion. I started travelling and encountering more foreigners and I felt a strong desire to understand them and communicate with them.

When I was studying my first degree in translation and interpreting, little by little I started to develop a method that enabled me to learn languages in a much more efficient way than before. I also started learning multiple languages at the same time. It was not a conscious decision, I just did it because I wanted to learn the languages of the people I encountered.

Languages allow me to get to know wonderful people that I would never otherwise have met because of the language barrier. Languages create new experiences and offer a better understanding of the world – a world made up of people who don't necessarily speak English or my mother tongue, which is Italian.

Learning languages allows me to read (or listen to) interesting content in different languages without needing translations and to understand the cultures and mentalities behind them. I really enjoy having a better understanding of why people use certain words and what people really mean when they speak another language.

My passion for languages, as well as my determination, has helped me find my own way through the complex process of learning foreign languages and I want to share what I have learnt with you in order to help you do the same.

If you are reading this, you have probably learnt one or more languages but would like to learn even more and are wondering whether multilingual learning is something for you and whether it works. Or, maybe you are interested in learning more than one language but aren't sure if it's a good idea to learn them at the same time and maybe you think that you aren't any good at learning languages. Whatever the case, I would like you to know: it's NOT you, just the way you were taught or told how to learn languages. With the right method ANYONE can learn languages and even more than one at the same time!

I am certain that **anyone** can learn multiple foreign languages at the same time. I base my belief on twenty years of experience as a language teacher, during which I have never met someone who could not learn a language.

In most cases, people simply believe that they are no good at languages, maybe because they didn't get good marks in their language classes at school, or because they feel like their progress isn't quick enough. In fact, what is often forgotten is that **almost anything we want to learn can be easy or difficult depending on the method used (self-study or with the teacher)**. I believed I was rubbish at chemistry in school until we had a substitute teacher for two weeks in Year 11, and for the first time ever not only did I understand some chemistry, but I actually enjoyed the classes a lot!

The sad part is that I meet people on a daily basis who wish they could speak a certain language (often more than one) and who truly believe that they are no good at languages or that a certain language is too difficult (in general or for them). On the contrary, what makes me incredibly happy is to see the smile on their face when after just five or ten minutes of a free lesson on the spot they realise that they CAN learn ANY language. I often do this little 'demonstration' because I love helping people and above all making them see their true potential. I love languages and it makes me very sad to see what traditional teaching has done to them.

Also, I was much more insecure in the past and now it makes me happy to contribute, even just a little bit, to people overcoming their fears. This is why my website is called 'speakfromdayonewithelisa'. I truly enjoy making learning not only possible but also fun and interactive from the very first moment. This is also the reason why when I give my demonstration or give multilingual workshops around the world, I choose languages that are considered to be difficult. If people can speak a difficult language like Hindi, Arabic, Russian or Greek from the very first moment, they can definitely speak any other language.

I also often hear people saying that they are no good at languages, because they tried to learn using flashcards made by people, who, for some strange reason, decided that teaching all the fruits in a beginners' course would help them progress in their language learning or that teaching long and difficult to pronounce words wouldn't put learners off and make them believe they have terrible pronunciation. Often, they also use language apps or language software that promise to teach you languages. In reality, these apps only give the *impression* that you are reaching an incredible level within a certain language, but when it comes to speaking, you can't build your own sentences (and the fact that many of the words used in these apps aren't useful for conversations doesn't help).

Or I meet people who are attending or have attended classes but are not able to say much at all. Many of them say that the teacher spoke more of their mother tongue than the target language, that classes were very boring or that the learning pace was either too quick or too slow for them.

I still remember with horror the worst class I ever saw. A famous and expensive language school told me that if I wanted to work there, I would have to observe one of their best English teachers so that I could use the same method. It was supposed to be an upper-intermediate class.

Can you believe that in the 90-minute class the students didn't say more than 'yes' or 'no'?! The teacher did more than 95% of the talking and was only talking about his life. He would ask: 'Did you have a good weekend?', 'yes', and he would go around asking the same question to every student (and he would encourage every student to say no more than 'yes'/'no'). On the rare occasions when he asked other questions during the class, he would ask something like 'where did you go on holiday?', and as soon as the answer was 'mmm, I went to Italy, and... mmm...', he would switch to another person. In a good class, the students talk a lot. If you don't get the chance to speak during a class, when are you supposed to speak and feel free to make mistakes (as everyone around you is in learning just like you)? No wonder people think they can't speak a language: they aren't even given the opportunity to speak in a situation in which they are actually paying to do so. Speaking is the only skill you can't really practise on your own (in theory it's possible, but it's not usually much fun).

A teacher should also encourage your learning, for instance by making something complicated easier to understand (but suitable for the level). For example, in Italian and French, one of the words for 'teacher' is 'insegnante'/'einsegnant', which means 'person who shows (the way)'.

All of this is strictly linked to a widely-debated and important topic that will be discussed in Part 5: '**With or without a teacher?**'. For now, I just would like to stress that it's almost always a matter of method. Our teacher or we can make the learning process efficient and fun according to the method that we (in the case of self-study) or our teacher decide to use.

Everyone is different and enjoys learning in different ways. The method and the learning strategies I describe in this book come from years of experience as both a learner and a teacher, and have worked for hundreds of people. With the help of my method, I know you can learn multiple languages. You may also want to consider customising my method with tricks that work for you or by adding in other activities that you enjoy. At the same time, although everything we learn will be useful in the end, the majority of your learning activities should focus on the skills that are most important to you. For example, if your main aim is speaking and you spend most of your study time reading, it will take you much longer to reach your goal. If instead your aim is to improve your understanding, you could choose any listening activity according to your preferences (videos, podcasts, music, news, etc.)

If you want to improve all your language skills, balance your language learning with different types of activities.

Having said that, if you go on holiday and you can only take a book with you, don't worry, it won't matter much if it's just for a couple of days. But in the long term, you should concentrate on the activities which bring you closer to your goals, because these are the activities that motivate us, and which bring results (and we are all motivated by results).

I will describe my method and effective learning strategies in detail in Part 5.

Your previous experience as a learner is more than valuable

Now I would like you to think for a moment about something that you wanted to learn and succeeded in doing. It can be anything, for example, riding a bike, writing, drawing, or playing an instrument. You may think of a subject at school you felt you were good at, or something you learnt for your job, or if your current job is new to you. Have you ever learnt the lyrics to a song, how to play a certain game or how to use an application on your smartphone? I bet you have! This means that at some point in your life you have definitely learnt something, and I am sure that now you can think of more than just one thing.

What were the common elements that led you to learn those activities? Maybe it was the **time** you dedicated to them, or your interest in them. Even if you felt obliged to learn them, perhaps because of your parents or because you needed a job, you were somehow **motivated** (for example so as not to disappoint your parents or in order to perform your job well). If it was your choice, you probably had some kind of **reward** for being able to do those activities, which could have simply been that it was fun or satisfying from a learning perspective. You might have to understand how best to learn them: maybe you figured it out by yourself or through a teacher or someone who could help you, and when you felt discouraged at times, **you did not give up** because you did eventually learn them. Even when it wasn't easy, you kept trying: how many times have we tried out the same movements, for example, when learning how to ride a bike?

Last but not least, because in a way it includes the elements we have just seen above, you used a **method**, even if you weren't actually aware of this. This method allowed you to learn.

For example, to learn the lyrics to your favourite song, you would have had to repeat them several times, while in other situations, you probably used other sources to understand something that wasn't clear. In some cases, you probably had good or at least decent material to help you learn, someone gave you some tips or advice or you watched a tutorial or a YouTube video.

Now think of something that you would like to learn.

Imagine achieving your goal.

How would you feel?

Imagine that for a moment.

What would you do then?

Other stories, your story

When I met my student Christopher for the first time, he was 35. He is German and works as programmer in an international company. His wife is Spanish, and they would speak English at home, as he couldn't speak Spanish and she couldn't speak German. Even though this worked for them, when visiting her family, he realised he had to rely on translations and couldn't speak directly with his in-laws. Although they were nice to him, he felt frustrated with not being able to connect with them. So, once he got home, he decided to start learning Spanish, but was concerned with mixing it up with French, a language that he was already learning for work. He reached out to me explaining his situation and first I helped him overcome his fear and then reach his goals. During our first lesson, he was already able to say so much more than he could when trying on his own. Just a couple of months later he could speak Spanish with his in-laws for the first time and he finally felt at home there. He didn't want to disappoint anyone, so he took Spanish lessons without telling his in-laws: her family was so happy and impressed, and once back home they started to speak Spanish at home.

Sofia is an Italian nurse who used to live in a place where job opportunities in her field are limited. She realised that by knowing other languages, she would have been able to move abroad and use her knowledge to help people in a different country, while having a more stable contract and maybe a better income. She was dithering about whether or not to move to Germany or to France, so she started taking German and French lessons with me. Six months later, she moved to Germany for her first job and a year later, she moved to Switzerland, where her French skills were instrumental in finding her position.

Their stories may well be similar to your own or to that of somebody you know. So this is what happens with languages. Once people learn languages, they open new doors for themselves or achieve a personal goal, such as being able to establish connections with members of their family. Everyone who learns a foreign language is a person like you, what is special about them is not a hidden talent for languages, but rather the fact that they succeeded because the method they are using is suited to them and aligned with their expectations. And with the right method, learning more than one language is totally doable. You may wonder whether learning multiple languages is time consuming: the method I am talking about has to do with **what you focus on** while learning and **how often** you learn. Quantity plays a role too, but what you do to learn is much more important than **how long** you study for. This is why it is much more important to perform a useful activity and do it five minutes a day than study once a week or every two weeks for a couple of hours. Focusing on the right things will help you make quicker progress and look back with satisfaction at all you have learnt and all you are already able to say in a short period of time.

Am I too old to learn languages?

I would like to address another point here. Very often I hear people saying they can't learn languages because they are too old, or that kids are better language learners. Neither or these statements are true: one can learn a language at any age and adults can learn even better than kids.

First of all, it is scientifically proven that although one may have better pronunciation if exposed to the language under the age of six, it is possible to have good pronunciation later on in life too. For some reason, many people think that they need to achieve a native level of pronunciation. Of course, very good pronunciation is important in some professions, such as interpretation, but not everyone wants to be a NATO interpreter. Can you think of a time a foreigner spoke to you in a language with a bit of an accent but with a very good level of the language? I imagine that they were able to understand and be understood perfectly, right? Did their accent impede communication? I have met so many people who spoke amazingly well but who didn't sound 100% as native speakers. Did it matter? Not at all. They perform very well in all situations and this is what matters. **Of course, pronunciation is important, but the main goal is communication**. It's not a pronunciation contest! And let's be honest, in some cases accents are cute or help create a conversation topic!

Think about the number of foreigners you have heard speaking your mother tongue well, at a level so high that you couldn't say if they were foreigners or not. Most likely this number is very small. **Even professional interpreters often have a foreign accent, but this does not prevent them from doing well professionally**.

So, unless you want to work as a spy, and in that case, I am afraid your pronunciation must be perfect (after all, it's a question of life or death!), your best will be good enough. And this is doable at any age. What makes kids different from adults is that, in most cases, kids are less afraid to try. Or, in many cases, they learn new languages at international schools while living abroad or because a parent only speaks to them in a certain language. Let's be honest, even if they are afraid, they don't have much choice. At school, teachers will talk to them in that language, as well as their parents and everyone else, around them if they are living abroad. Of course, one of the most natural environments for kids to learn languages in is when hanging out with friends who speak to them in other languages.

For adults, it sounds so easy: 'kids learn very quickly'. But wouldn't you also learn a language if you were put in a situation in which the only way to communicate was by using a language you didn't understand at all at the beginning?!

And why quickly? It take kids years before they become fluent in their first language. When living abroad, it normally takes them around a year to perform well at school if they didn't speak the language beforehand – year in which they were fully immersed in the language several hours a day, without the chance of speaking their mother tongue. Surely you would perform more or less in the same way under the same conditions?!

And when it comes to kids, there are important limits: when things aren't so fun, they immediately lose their motivation. In comparison, **adults can focus on their goals for longer periods of time in situations where they have to tolerate the absence of fun**. For example, I really enjoy walking and connecting with people when it's sunny out. I can meet my friends or make new ones. However, I am writing now because I believe I can help people and it means a lot to me. I am sure you have a busy life, but we can always make time for something which matters to us. Maybe not as much time as we would have liked, but if something means a lot to us, we will squeeze it in somehow.

Moreover, **adults know their own language better, and this helps them for many reasons, for example to establish comparisons with the target languages. Adults can establish a routine and follow it with a high level of awareness**, develop their own learning process and use all their background to make connections of any kind with things they already know. Their experience helps the brain establish more useful connections and learn faster. Whereas kids do not normally have a real interest in languages, adults are more aware of their interests and will work much harder to attain their goals. If all of this isn't enough to convince you that you can learn as many languages as you want at any age, let me remind you of something that I confessed in the previous part of this book...something that may change your mind: I learnt all the languages I speak, apart from one, after the age of 20!

Part 3

What does learning multiple languages at the same time mean?

Does learning multiple languages at the same time mean that we will say a word in one language and a different word in another? Of course not! Learning more than one language at the same time means: a) having separate moments for each language (you still want to speak one language at a time), b) comparing languages so that you have a clear idea of their unique or recurrent features (very important if you want to keep those languages separate in your brain and speed up your language learning process), and c) having moments where you switch between languages (in order to get used to this switching so that you can speak multiple languages without mixing them up!).

You can do all of this on your own, using the method and learning strategies described throughout this book and especially in Part 5. I have been doing so for years as there were no multilingual courses or multilingual teachers, and it works very well. I'm sure that if you follow the steps described in this book, you will do wonderfully!

Other possible options are multilingual lessons and/or multilingual courses, both as additional resources for your self-study.

The big advantage is that you can train all your languages in one session and you learn how not to mix them up. For example, my students train up to 3 languages in a 60-minute session and up to 6 languages in a 90-minute session, and after two or three sessions, they almost never mix languages up.

In my multilingual classes, for example, students learn all their favourite languages in an extremely effective and interactive way and start speaking them from the very beginning, without mixing languages up. Any language combination is possible, and it is also possible to combine languages that you have different levels in. The point isn't to say the same thing in all languages but to use all the languages to talk about your life and interests.

I also recently published the very first online multilingual course. I designed the course because I wanted to offer reliable and fun learning material to multilingual learners who want to study on their own but also want a course based on learning strategies and a multilingual method that really work. In these courses, I applied exactly what I described at the beginning of Part 3: first you start learning one language and then, shortly afterwards, you add in the other languages one by one. The huge difference between my method and monolingual courses is that the languages are interconnected in my courses: language features are explained in detail, multilingual tips and language learning tips are highlighted in each single-language unit.

I know that learning languages is achieved more quickly when using different channels, this is why my course includes multilingual podcasts, videos, speaking practice, flashcards with only useful words, grammar summaries with useful words and example, short stories and much more.

However you decide to learn (or improve) your languages, I am sure that if you follow the easy steps described in this book, you will succeed and speak them confidently.

Which languages to choose and how many languages at the same time (max)

If you want to start learning multiple languages at the same time, you may wonder how many languages can be learnt together and whether there is a magic number, or a maximum. Success in learning multiple languages depends on various factors. We discussed motivation in the previous sections, and we will talk even more about it in the last chapter, but it goes without saying that one should learn multiple languages at the same time only if there is real motivation to do so. Most people already know what languages they would like to study but they have some doubts about a) the number (whether they should/could add more languages or whether they should reduce the number) and b) their combination.

In fact, any number and combination is possible, but your ideal combination depends on various factors and especially on your motivation and on your free time at that particular moment in your life.

If it's true that learning multiple languages at the same time is in no way proportional to the number of languages and that it is possible to learn them in almost the same amount of time you would learn one (of course with the right method), remember that we have to work for it just like anything else that we would like to learn in life. Depending on your goals and internal or external deadlines, even five minutes a day of self-study per language could be enough – even five minutes per five languages is doable. But for more than that or for more languages – I even studied up to 13 at the same time – it will be much more challenging because a daily routine should be established and reasonably sustained throughout the whole learning period.

Then of course, if your aim is speaking, you should also train that.

The limiting factor is usually time. First of all, the time they can spend learning every day is limited and, second, they want to achieve a certain level in a limited amount of time. Of course, the strength of motivation has an effect on this, because we think we are very busy, but we can always make time for things which are relevant to us. The equation is, therefore, rather straightforward: the time available for learning every single day determines the maximum number of languages, given that a minimum of five minutes a day is mandatory to establish a successful routine. My students usually pick a number of languages between three and five, which is generally what I recommend. There is no magic behind this number, it simply comes from the fact that you can usually spend between one and two hours every day doing homework. If more than this is required, people tend to lose motivation, slow down or even give up.

We usually end up with a reasonable number of languages to learn.

Therefore, learning multiple languages at the same time is not as time consuming as you may think.

In fact, you do not need lots of time per day to learn a language, five minutes is enough! Yes, it is! And everyone has five minutes a day, it's just a matter of wanting it.

Many people think that learning a language means studying many hours a day. Of course, the more (quality) inputs, the quicker you can learn. However, if you don't have much time, I really believe that it is much better to study five minutes a day than two hours every week or even less frequently. Especially if a language is new for us, our memory needs short learning intervals to remember things and to connect the things we learn.

Apart from that, if you study every two weeks or even more frequently you won't see much progress, and this will demotivate you. If the method or system you follow is what gives you results, your motivation is what will help you stick to it. If you walked every day for 15 minutes do you know how many miles you would have walked in one year? Now compare that to language learning. Even if you learnt three words a day, after one year you would already have enough vocabulary to have conversations in most languages (for example, studies show that you need around 500 words to talk and be understood in everyday situations when speaking Italian, in English you need around 800 words).

When I say five minutes, of course I am not talking about needing to learn a language within a very short time frame. If you want to be able to have conversations about different topics in let's say one week, you will need to study much more. However, if you have a realistic goal, five minutes a day can be enough (but of course you may want to study more if you want to make quicker progress). I will go into more detail about this later on in this book.

Another relevant aspect to setting the number of languages you start to learn is their initial level. You don't have to have the same level in all the languages you study – although, if you are a beginner in all them, this would make your life easier because you will learn similar tenses and structures in all your languages, which will speed up your learning process, and you will need to memorise similar vocabulary, which will be done with much less effort for similar languages. It will also help you to simplify what you want to say. Because you have a relatively small vocabulary, you will learn how to simplify your sentences so that you are understood and doing this for one language will help you with the others (because at a beginner level we mostly talk about our life and interests, so the topics will be similar).

Moreover, it will help you to compare similar languages and understand language features – this is very important for learning how not to mix languages up.

If you are a beginner in one or more languages and intermediate or advanced in the other(s), it definitely works too! The advantages of combining languages of which you have different levels are: a) speaking in the language you can already speak well will help you remind yourself that you CAN reach language fluency and this will improve your confidence, very beneficial when we want to learn new things (we are often our toughest critics!), b) if the language you already know is similar to the one(s) you want to learn from scratch, it will help you improve more quickly because you will find many similarities, and c) if the language is different, the language training will still pass to your other language(s) in terms of training the brain, in the same way that learning any new musical instrument is aided by the knowledge of other instruments even when they are quite different. In fact, if your level in one language is different to that in another language, you will certainly do different activities according to the level, and the more you experiment and have fun with a language, the better a learner you will become by improving your method and understanding what works best for you.

Part 4

Routine v willpower

There are many ways to learn languages, but making steady progress requires self-discipline and a daily routine (even if it's studying for just 5 to 10 minutes a day). You need self-discipline to get started and <u>establish</u> a routine, but once you have a routine, things will be much easier, and you will need very little conscious willpower to stick to your routine.

A language routine is important because we would follow it almost automatically, with very little conscious effort. I remember when I first learnt how to drive a manual car. I had to think of so many things at once: check for other vehicles nearby, or pedestrians who want to cross the road or get out of their cars without first looking around, steer, change gears, remember the route, etc.

On top of this, talking, changing the radio station or turning on the air conditioning while taking into consideration all of the above seemed impossible and was very overwhelming. Nowadays, having had lots of practice, I'm not even aware that I'm doing so many things at once! And this goes for all of our routines: do you remember EXACTLY how you brushed your teeth this morning? As children, we had to learn how to do it! Do you have to think long and hard about the way home from work or school? It's the same when cooking, eating, and for many of our tasks at work, etc. We do them without thinking about them and without struggling: we already know what to do.

This is why routine is so important: you just do it.

Routine comes AFTER willpower. Things that require willpower often require lots of effort because we have to consider whether we feel tired, frustrated, upset, etc. In the morning, I always do some sit-ups. At the beginning, it was hard, especially on days when I felt tired or was in a hurry, let alone first thing in the morning. Now I don't even think about it, I just do it.

The more effort something requires and is dependent on my mental and physical state, the more aware I am of the need to build a routine. And even when it **seems** 'impossible', it's only 'impossible' until you actually do it. Once you've started, you realise how easy it is.

If you have already tried to build a routine but haven't found an efficient way to keep it up in order to achieve your goals, you will find many useful tips, insights and practical ways to build your language routine here (in Part 4) and in Part 5 (the most practical part of this book). These tips and insights have worked (and still work!) for me and for hundreds of people.

Even if you are a well-disciplined person, I still suggest you read this section and see if you can further improve your language learning skills.

The right mental state

Another key factor in building a routine that we can stick to is our **mental state**. The right mental state helps us a) build our routine (for example, by helping us feel less intimidated by what lies ahead and look at it from a different perspective, or by helping us enjoy our language learning activities more, which will enable us to stick to our routine each day and make it a habit), b) stay motivated (with the right mental state, we believe in what we are doing and know that we will see results) and c) make more progress (with the right mental state, we absorb more information).

What is the right mental state? This relates to focusing on the moment and on what we can do instead of on things that are out of our control or that we wish were different. Focusing on the moment is a concept that can be applied to any activity in our lives, but for the purpose of this book, let's just focus on what we are doing while we are learning languages. If we concentrate on what we are doing, shutting out our worries and above all our **negative inner talk** (e.g. 'I'm not good enough', 'I'm bad at languages', 'It's too difficult for me', 'I'll never be able to learn this', 'It will take me ages', 'I have bad pronunciation', etc.), we will be able to absorb the information better, at least during our study session. How do you expect to stay motivated with such negative thoughts running through your head?

A quote I like states: "If someone spoke to you in the same way that you sometimes talk to yourself, how long would you stay friends with that person?!" Besides, it's normally when we focus 100% on what we are doing that we are in our 'flow state' and enjoy ourselves the most, and such a positive state is necessary to create and keep up our habit.

An example of how our mental state plays an important role is when people start learning a new language. They are normally very motivated, but sooner or later they find themselves in front a **steep mountain**. Not because learning a language must be complicated, but because the learning curve is gentler at the beginning than at later stages, as everything is new and generally much easier. For instance, it is much easier to learn a couple of words or short sentences and speak very slowly than to start building more complex sentences and speaking at a normal speed.

Normally, the more we learn, the more we understand that there is still a lot to learn, and this can be overwhelming. It may seem like the top of the mountain is a long way away and being able to say 'I made it' seems like an impossibility. The trick is to take things one step at a time. It's the same with languages as well as with any other long task, such as a big project at work or writing a dissertation: **get started and little by little you will start to see progress, and eventually you will make it**.

This is often what prevents people from starting to learn a language or building a routine.

If they haven't started to learn a language, the path in front of them might discourage them, and they forget by taking things one step at a time, NOTHING is impossible.

If they have started but are having trouble establishing their routine, often it's because they are waiting for the 'right moment' (which normally never comes) and because they imagine that they have to work on languages for several hours a day to see some progress. When something similar happened to me, I realised that if I had started when I was first interested in learning that particular language and had studied just one word a day, my vocabulary would have been HUGE by now.

Even when we don't have time, one small step at a time will keep us moving forward. Similarly, taking our mental state into consideration, focusing on what we CAN do right now (instead of what we can't do) will help us get even closer to our goals.

Treat yourself kindly: a healthy mental state promotes success

Something important that is too often forgotten is creating a mental state towards success. As adults, we often forget that we were all students once: we can perform normally in our daily lives, but when it comes to speaking a new language, we feel as if we know nothing and it's frustrating. We expect to know everything, and we may even get angry with ourselves for not remembering words or for not performing as we well as we think we could.

Bear in mind that you are in a learning phase and as such you simply cannot know or remember everything. Learning is a beautiful experience: it makes us leave our comfort zone, and it can be very rewarding. When we are stressed, we don't think clearly: how can we perform well if we treat ourselves worse than how we treat good friends? Our mental state matters. So, be open to learning, be kind to yourself and be aware that this is a path we all have to go down if we want to improve and grow.

Practical tips to help you with your routine

Let's say that you've started to create your routine but one day (usually during the first few weeks), you are intimidated by how much work there is ahead of you. Perhaps it's a **long study session** or an **ambitious language goal** we set for ourselves that day, or maybe it's our long-term language goal that for some reason seems further away than it usually does. If this happens to you, it is really important that before starting your **daily routine**, you go through a short preparation phase, during which you get into the right state of mind. One of the activities I recommend is moving your body a bit, such as taking a short walk, light stretching or simply breathing deeply for a minute to give your brain a break from previous activities or thoughts, so that it's ready to absorb new information.

The correct **state of mind** creates the basis for us to believe in what we are doing and, if combined with daily work (even just a short learning session), we will see very positive results.

Set a reachable and defined goal: step approach v mountain

Setting reachable goals is important. Have you ever set an unrealistic goal that you couldn't stick to and decided to avoid the stress? This is what happens to many people, not only when learning languages.

A good way to approach this may be to have a vision (your ultimate goal and why), and then work on concrete goals. If these goals are still quite big, then think in terms of steps.

Take things one step at a time and you will definitely be closer to your goal.

Sometimes we are too hard on ourselves and want too much, too soon. A quote I like states: "If you think your destination is far away, get started and think about it as you walk". Don't look at the mountain in front of you, concentrate on the small steps which will take you closer to what you want to achieve. Even the furthest goal is just a matter of steps away.

State of mind, motivation and results

I don't know about you but many people, including me, are motivated by results. I can study, go on a diet and so on, but if I don't see results, I get discouraged. On the one hand, we are living in an age in which we need results now, and we don't want to wait. Take the famous three-second clicking rule, for instance: most of us won't wait for longer than three seconds for a webpage to load before moving our search elsewhere. Think of all the things we can obtain just through a simple click and it's not difficult to see why we have become so impatient. On top of that, most people have also forgotten what learning means: trying out a method, being consistent and patient, and knowing that on some days we will do better than on other days.

Have you ever seen children really interested in something and giving up immediately? It may happen from time to time, but children are normally able to pick something up and stick with it for a large amount of time. Take piano playing for instance. Children can play the same keys for hours if they enjoy it (or if they have to). They don't usually look too far ahead and they don't think: "If I keep doing it at this pace, I will never become a pianist".

When I was a teenager, I really wanted to learn the piano. Unfortunately, I couldn't take lessons, so I decided to learn on my own. Then, I asked a friend at a party to show me how to play 'Für Elise', a classical piece by Beethoven which I really liked. At school, I had learnt the flute at a very basic level, and I didn't know how to write or read the music. I wrote the notes in my own way and trained for hours and hours (at the party but also at my grandmother's house later that evening). I never tired of playing the same bits over and over again because I was working on something that meant a lot to me. Now when I listen to the recording of me playing, I still feel incredibly happy because it reminds me of those moments when nothing but music and my goal existed. Focus on what you are doing and don't think too far ahead, you will get there!

I also remember trying to learn the same dance steps for hours and hours and I never thought I was wasting my time or felt bad because I couldn't get them right straight away.

As adults, we tend to forget that learning anything worthwhile takes time. For many people, it has been a long time since they learnt something new. In any case, we are becoming more and more used to the immediate reward. As adults, we often get frustrated if we can't speak a language fluently from the very beginning or don't understand every single word people say. In particular, this happens to people who haven't learnt a new language for a long time because they forgot that learning is a journey. Even when we see a mountain before us, we should remember that without action, there can be no results, but a small action can bring results.

Our mental state is important because it isn't possible to absorb much if we feel frustrated. It's important to treat ourselves kindly. We are often our own worst critics, expecting too much and too soon. I still remember when I was trying to learn a German sound ('ch', meaning 'ich'), and I knew it wasn't perfect. I got very frustrated and it didn't help. Even after trying hard in that moment, I just couldn't do it. Then one day, I was spending time with some German friends and it just came out of my mouth!

Work towards your goals with a peaceful mental state. Thinking about something that we need or want to finish can be frustrating. However, tackling it one step at a time is one of the most effective ways of making us believe in ourselves and pushing ourselves forward.

Motivation: how to keep going

A common problem when studying languages is the loss of motivation. Normally it happens because we are not reaching an anticipated result.

Sometimes we can't see our progress because languages are systems, and unless we use an efficient method, it may take longer to see how the things we learn are connected. Sometimes the method we are using is not the right one to help us reach our goal. As I always say: if your aim is speaking and you never speak, you cannot expect to be fluent the first time you decide to speak (unless you do lots of productive written exercises that activate the same part of the brain needed for speaking, such as creating sentences or texts).

Setting goals that are too ambitious can also demotivate us. For example, if we decide that we want to be fluent in one month (or two, three or six months, or one year, etc.), it MIGHT be possible to reach that goal, but the tighter the deadline, the more we should plan. Results depend on how different your native language is to the target language, the language(s) you already know, the exposure to the language, the time you invest in it and, above all, the method and strategies you use. How can you plan your language learning? How can you find an efficient method that works for you? You can choose the right language materials, set speaking practice moments and follow the many strategies and tips explained in this book.

Remember to set a reasonable goal for the deadline you set for yourself. A goal is made of many small steps, so try to split them up according to the number of days available in order to see if the goal is feasible or if something should be changed (by doing more every day, setting yourself a more realistic goal or by giving yourself more time).

Think about you and your life and consider what you can do every day to get closer to your goal. It is very important to have feasible daily goals, otherwise you will soon lose motivation. Remember that it is much better to do a little bit every day than a lot once a week (also because most people won't get around to 'a lot every week' for one reason or another). If your daily goal is too ambitious, you will soon feel frustrated. If it is a more feasible goal, you will feel good about yourself and most likely try to do a bit more. We are driven by results: when we see that we are succeeding in something important to us, we invest more energy it.

You can also choose to have a multilingual mentor, a language coach or (multilingual) teacher to help you. I help language learners set feasible goals, build their routine, reach fluency, feel more confident, have fun with the language and, if they are learning multiple languages, avoid mixing them up. For example, I created a useful language learning planner to help you set your goals, stay motivated and get a bit closer to your goals each day.

A professional language teacher, mentor or coach can

show you that what you have already done IS important but also show you what else you can do to reach the next level in your language learning process. For example, by helping you use the many words you have already learnt and by teaching you language structures suitable for your level.

I know many people who study words through apps but then cannot use them in conversations. This is completely normal and, again, with the right method, you can build up from what you already know. Everything we have learnt will come handy in the end, we just have to find the right method to combine it with useful and tailored strategies and language structures. If you aren't there yet, you are only a few steps away!

The past is the past: how do we succeed in the future?

Maybe you've tried to learn one or multiple languages before. Now is the time to think about what or who is preventing you from succeeding.

Have you lost your motivation? Maybe you felt that it was too difficult or that it wasn't worth the effort, or maybe you felt that you weren't learning as quickly as you would have liked. This is certainly something you can overcome with the right method or system.

Of course, you have to want it and believe in it. Staying motivated is easy at first but can get more difficult after the first few days.

Another reason might be that you set an unrealistic goal that you couldn't keep up with and you decided to avoid the stress. The reason for wanting to learn something can differ greatly from person to person, but if your goal is to be fluent in four weeks, just in time for your holiday, and you tell yourself that you have to study seven days a week and you already have a tight schedule, you're probably going to give up. Sometimes we are just too hard on ourselves and don't show ourselves enough patience or kindness.

If there is a language you have always wanted to learn or that you started learning and then stopped, you can start (again) today! With the right method, you can do it!

With the right method, anyone can learn a language.

Something important that many adults forget is what it means to learn something new. For many people, school is a distant memory and not being able to express themselves in another language (as they can in their mother tongue or any other language they are fluent in) makes them uncomfortable. Many people get frustrated by this and forget that it took them between one and five years to learn a language at school, sometimes even longer. Moreover, many school syllabi are structured in a way that makes it very difficult for students to become fluent in a foreign language. In some cases, they know the grammar very well, but they can't speak the language. In other cases, students don't even have a sound grasp of the grammar.

It's also got a lot to do with the method we used or the way we were taught the language. Nowadays, however, with all the resources available, you don't need five years to learn a language and you can certainly start speaking from the very first day (if you don't expect to know everything at first, of course). You can find videos on speaking a language from the very first moment without having any previous knowledge of it on my website .

Would you like to be able to do this too? First, you'll need the right method, mental approach and material (some of these were discussed above, but you will read more about them in subsequent sections). Then, you'll need to overcome your fear of making mistakes at the beginning. If you feel that making mistakes is what is stopping you, then I suggest you work with a teacher or a language coach to help you overcome this fear.

Additionally, be aware that studies show that there are learning sequences (things that our brain can understand and use correctly at the beginning and other things which come later). This is one of the reasons why most people find it overwhelming to learn one rule and all the exceptions at the same time: it is much better to learn something, apply it, play with it and go back to it in more detail later. A bit like an onion, we learn best through layers. It is also important not to be too hard on yourself, enjoy it! You will get there!

Our mental state is important: you have to believe that it's possible. There are so many experiments and evidence that prove that our performance is better when we believe in ourselves and visualise the outcome (more details in Part 5). What you need to get started is motivation, hope and a realistic goal. What you need to continue is a method or system which helps you build up a routine and offer positive results.

Now let's talk about your goals. Many people wish they could either be totally fluent in a language or at least be able to get by while travelling. To set a realistic goal, think about what you actually want to do with the language you want to learn: do you live abroad and want to integrate more? Or do you like to share things about yourself while travelling and want to arrange to meet up with a local during the evening?

Do we really need to be totally fluent? You don't need to be 'perfect' to enjoy a conversation. Communication is not about how well you speak, but rather what you transmit. Even more important is being able to avoid cultural mistakes, which could have an impact on your interaction, even if you're not aware of it. I'm not saying that you shouldn't speak a language at an advanced level, just that you can start to enjoy talking to people before reaching that level. If your aim is talking to people and you start speaking and communicating from the beginning, the very act of using the language and vocabulary will keep you motivated.

If you have studied the language before, the good thing is that everything you have learnt, even if you think you don't remember anything, will come back to you. You will need much less time to recall what you knew compared to the time you spent learning it. Neurologists say that it would be good if you used the same material you used in the past (especially your own notes or material), because the synapses have already been built and picking the language up again will be much quicker.

Motivation is what gets us started, but habit is what keeps the ball rolling.

The truth is, when it comes to finding an hour a day for language learning, most people say that it's impossible. We all have busy schedules and it can seem impossible to fit any more in. Plus, an hour can sound intimidating. This is why I suggest you start with a much smaller amount of time.

What I personally do is choose a doable amount of time to start with: usually 5 to 30 minutes according to my schedule and goals. However, you will see that after some days, especially with the right method, material and/or tutor, you will want to learn more because you will see how much you are learning or because you are enjoying yourself. I usually stick to my 5-30 minutes rule, without exception, knowing that I have done at least the minimum amount (if we are motivated, finding five minutes a day is always possible), but if I can, I study/practise more. Of course, I am talking about five minutes a day without distraction!

Even people who hate routine perform most of their daily actions because of a routine: eating, taking a shower, brushing their teeth, calling someone, working, going somewhere, talking a certain route to work, etc. Even if you like change, like I do, a habit will help you start to do things automatically. What seemed difficult to start with will, after a certain number of days, become automatic and your brain will be craving it.

If you want to try out and keep track of your routine, I would suggest a great free app called Habitica (https://habitica.com). When I started out, I found it difficult to do even one or two things a day, but in very little time, I found that I could easily do 20 to thirty 30 things a day. This brings us to a very important topic: time.

I don't have time

Many people say that they don't have time. This is often true. However, the point isn't to have time but to make time! Luckily, there are very few cases in which unfortunate circumstances mean people have zero time – but even these cases don't usually affect every single day of a person's life.

When you think you don't have time, consider this: if they gave you £100,000 to study a language for 15 minutes a day for 30 days, do you think you could do that?

Most of the time wanting something badly enough will help you find the time. Everyone wastes time every day. To give you an idea of how much time you waste on a daily basis, try to keep track of how much time you spend on your smartphone. When I tried myself, I was shocked – I always thought that I spent my time wisely!

How much time do you spend on social media, commuting, or watching TV? What about doing something fun and useful while waiting for the bus or train? Many of us also waste time because we have to do a task that we either dislike or are afraid of and can't force ourselves to get started. This is just wasted time.

The best thing to do is just get started. The fear will remain until we start, but then it magically disappears. Being stuck too long doesn't help. In fact, it gives you a bad feeling. If you use your time wisely, you will feel better and more motivated in many areas of your life.

What do you normally do alongside doing the washing up or tidying your flat? You could listen to a podcast, radio channel or music in your target language. Maybe you could spend some time looking for good material and then enjoy it in your spare time. Having something prepared will help avoid you wasting time in the future, especially on your busiest days, because instead of thinking about what you could do, you can immediately start doing it. And if you think about it in advance, you can be sure that you will be watching, listening or studying something YOU like.

Even on days when you are really busy, you can do small things like: a) revise one or two notes from a lesson (only relevant words, verbs, expressions or language structures please!), b) listen to music in your favourite languages while working, driving or studying (more about passive learning in Part 5), c) write a very short message to a friend in a foreign language, d) sing along a (foreign) song you like (as well as you can, it doesn't have to be perfect), e) listen to a podcast for five minutes (only in the target language, and make them five effective minutes! I know many podcasts that say they will teach you a language but they spend most of the time speaking in English, which is not an optimal way to spend your time if you only have five minutes), or f) watch five minutes of a movie or series you like, or g) focus on a couple of words on your phone when set in the target language (not recommended for languages you don't understand much!).

The last example is not the best option if you are a beginner because you won't learn words that you can immediately use – but it's an option to keep you at it even on busy days. Anything little activity will help you along your learning path, so don't worry if you can't study as much as you would like. Step by step you will get there!

How can I find time?

When it comes to finding time for language learning, most people say it's impossible, especially if they have a long study session in mind. An hour a day, for example, can sound intimidating. We all have busy schedules and it can seem impossible to fit any more in.

This is why I suggest starting with a much smaller portion of time: start with at least five minutes a day, but without exception. If we are motivated, finding five minutes a day is always possible. Start small. The more progress you see and the more you enjoy your language learning, the more time you will want to dedicate to it. And this will require very little effort because it will be fun and rewarding.

If you know that it's hard for you to find time, don't start too big. If you do, you may get frustrated if you don't manage to do everything you wanted to do that day and you'll just give up. Remember, you can always increase the amount of study time as you progress.

Personally, what I do is choose a doable amount of time to start with: usually 5 to 30 minutes according to my schedule and goals. I usually stick to my 5-30 minutes rule, without exception, knowing that I have done at least the minimum amount (if we are motivated, finding five minutes a day is always possible), but if I can, I study/ practise more. Of course, I am talking about five minutes a day without distraction!

The most important thing is that you start. Once you get started, you should commit to studying and find what inspires you. Then, let the routine take the lead.

Keep track of your achievements on a regular basis. If you stick to the five-minute rule, it will be rewarding to see how disciplined you have been even after just one week, and you will feel (and be) closer to your goals.

When establishing your routine, it's very effective to think retrospectively about your day: what could you do better tomorrow to improve your learning experience?

Don't focus on what went wrong (for example, many things came up and you couldn't study), focus on what you could do better. For example, ask yourself, "What small thing could I change tomorrow in my routine implementation?" You may want to find a different place or time to study, so as not to get interrupted. Or maybe you decide to start your study routine with an activity you really enjoy, so that you are more inclined to begin.

Answering this question on a regular basis will help you establish a fair partnership with your learning method and routine and, at the same time, will give you a view of where you are compared to where you started and where you want to go. If we don't keep track of both our efforts and results, we tend to either overestimate or underestimate our situation.

My suggestion is: use a tool to help you with your evaluation of effort and results, or have a multilingual mentor or coach help you.

I really want you to reach your goals and enjoy your language learning, so I want to share with you a powerful tool that I use in my multilingual (and monolingual) mentoring (and coaching) sessions with my students. In the appendix of this book, you will find a link to my Language learning planner. It will help you set your daily and long-term goals and, above all, keep track of your achievements. It also contains motivational tips to accompany you on your journey and retrospective questions to help you improve your routine straight away.

Multilingual language mentoring and coaching

Next, I'd like to briefly clarify the difference between 'language mentoring' and 'language coaching', as there seems to be a lot of confusion around the terms and understanding the difference between them may help when identifying exactly what it is that you're looking for.

Are mentoring and coaching identical?

No. People often confuse mentoring and coaching. Though related, they are not the same.

Both language mentors and language coaches create a safe learning environment for taking risks (e.g. they help students overcome the fear of making mistakes when speaking) and help students leave their comfort zone in order to improve their performance.

So, what are the differences between mentoring and coaching?

What is mentoring?

Mentoring can be defined as a relationship in which an experienced person (the mentor) assists another (the student) in developing specific skills and knowledge. The mentor facilitates the student's language learning path by sharing resources and experience in their field of expertise (e.g. language learning, teaching, etc.). A mentor provides both professional and personal support and may give advice.

What is coaching?

Coaching supports the student's language learning path by prompting them to find their own method and path.

A language coach does not tell you what you must do but helps you to build your own learning system and customise it to fit your needs. In this way, a language coach helps you to find your own answers and what really works for you.

Coaching is based on concrete actions to improve the current learning stage.

Do I need a language mentor or a language coach?

The ICF (International Coach Federation) defines coaching as "partnering with clients in a thought-provoking and creative process that inspires them to maximize their personal and professional potential". This does not involve the transfer of knowledge, expertise or advice. According to this definition, a language coach uses coaching techniques to help you to find your own answers, motivation and path.

As a language mentor gives advice, shares their expertise and uses coaching techniques to assist students in learning a language or improving their language skills, what most people are really looking for is a language mentor or, even better, a language teacher who is also a language mentor. In the case of learning multiple languages at the same time, the best option would be a multilingual mentor.

As an alternative, you can sign up for or create your own accountability group, where language learners share their progress, achievements and struggles, so as to help and support each other. My students find my accountability groups very effective because these groups help them stick to their language learning routines.

Keeping track of your achievements and working on improving your language routine are very powerful activities which will boost your language learning. Sometimes we create our own obstacles, especially in our mind and through our habits. The good thing is that we can change both.

Now let's take a look at some useful language learning strategies and see how we can put everything that you've learnt so far into practice!

Part 5

How to learn multiple languages at the same time in a fun and efficient way

If you've read this far, you've probably already decided that you want to study multiple languages at the same time but would like more details on how to do so in an efficient and fun way. You probably want to know how it differs from studying one language at a time.

Let's first address that second point: how studying multiple languages at the same time differs from studying just one language at a time. Well, there are a certain number of common points but there are also some important differences.

Learning more than one language at the same time doesn't mean learning multiple languages in the same moment, at least not all the time (PHASE 1). Because you'll only really want to speak one language at a time in real life, you need to have separate moments for each language. The good thing is that you don't need to study each language for hours on end to see results.

Similar languages will help you progress at a quicker pace and different languages will give your brain a rest and help you train and improve your language skills in general (I talked about this in more detail in Part 2). What's most important is to study each language you want to learn a bit every day – even for just five minutes on busy days is enough. Of course, by five minutes I mean five minutes doing the things that help you the most, and with no distractions (more practical tips on this to follow in this section).

Studying a bit every day will a) help us remember what we learn (anyone would feel frustrated if they opened a book after two weeks and couldn't remember what they had learnt before!), b) help our brain make connections between the different bits of the language we have learnt, and c) help us stay motivated. If you only studied every two weeks, you wouldn't see much progress, and this would demotivate you.

Why not try to learn a language for a short period of time every day for 30 days and see the results? You can do it on your own and I'm sure that, by applying the many tips in this book, you will do wonderfully well!

If you would prefer to either be a part of a 30-day challenge group or have a customised program, completely tailored to your needs and your lifestyle (either with or without multilingual mentoring sessions and/or single-language or multilingual lessons), you can reach me through my website or through my Facebook page.

Going back to 'how' to study multiple languages: on one hand, it is important to study your languages separately even just for a little bit every day in an efficient way. On the other hand, you need to compare the languages so that you have a clear idea of their unique or recurrent features (PHASE 2). This is very important if you want to keep the languages separate in your brain and speed up your language learning process. I gave some practical examples about this in Part 2 and more will follow in this section.

During phases 1 and 2, focus on what's different. By this I mean that if something is similar in two languages, don't spend too much time on it. Instead, focus on the differences. For example, among Romance languages, lots of vocabulary and grammar rules are very similar but there will also be language-specific features, as well as exceptions. For example, in some Romance languages, there are two verbs for the English equivalent of the verb 'to be'. Additionally, in French and Italian, 'on Wednesdays' is expressed by using the singular article 'le mercredi'/'il mercoledì', whereas in Spanish you need the plural article 'los miercoles'. This is what you should focus on. As for the similarities between languages, what you know in one language can be applied to the others (e.g. how tenses and grammar points work etc.). This will speed up your learning process.

If you are studying similar languages, the aim is of course to be sure that what we say belongs to the correct language, and that that we are not mixing words of different languages up. But before we reach this point, there will be many situations in which we remember a word in one language but aren't sure whether the same word exists in another language. When this happens, we can try to find the root through our knowledge of language features. It's usually something quite similar.

An example: if we know the verb 'pensar' ('to think' in Spanish) and we know how infinitive verb forms (the basic forms of verbs found in dictionaries) end in Italian, we might guess 'pensare' in Italian, and we would be right! We could also remember that the most common infinitive ending in French is 'er' ('ar' does not exist in French verbs), so we would guess 'penser'.

As far as pronunciation is concerned, we would just apply what we already know: pronounce all the letters in Italian (only very few exceptions exist) and, in French, pronounce 'en' as 'a/a/' followed by a nasal 'n' sound and never pronounce the 'r' in '-er' infinitive forms (yes, French has many more pronunciation rules).

Sometimes we will guess incorrectly. For example, the

equivalent expressions for 'of course' in Spanish, Italian and French are quite different ('por supuesto', 'certo' and 'bien sûr'), and sometimes it may lead to us saying something funny. I love those moments! I know that I will remember these phrases forever and I will have a funny story to tell!

It's also important to have moments in which you switch between languages to get used to speaking multiple languages without mixing them up (PHASE 3)!

You can of course practise them separately and, if you do this often enough, it will also work. As I mention in Part 2, it's not a case of speaking one language much more than the others, otherwise you would have the tendency to speak THAT language when you actually want to speak the other one(s). If you speak them regularly without neglecting any that you want to be able to improve, you will learn not to mix them up.

The 'perfect' frequency depends on several factors, for example on whether you have a higher level in one of the languages. The higher the level, the less often you need to speak it in order to maintain or improve it. In any case, if you are at a beginner level or low intermediate, I would suggest that you speak the languages at least once a week (the more the better, of course).

Speaking is a difficult skill to train by yourself (unless you enjoy talking to yourself aloud, which I sometimes do, but I personally find it boring after a couple of minutes).

I try to find as many ways as possible to speak. It can be a group language exchange, or a two-people language exchange. I don't normally rely on friends unless I already speak the language very well, because I don't want to bore them – and they are my friends because I love talking to them and doing activities together, and I can't expect them to speak at 'turtle speed' or to repeat everything several times.

With or without a teacher?

Personally, I enjoy studying with AND without a teacher. Having studied languages for over 20 years, and being a passionate teacher myself, I know how I need a teacher to be. If the teacher can help me with what I am looking for, I am more than happy to study with them. If a teacher is not passionate about what they do and they don't adapt to what a student really needs in order to improve, then I prefer to study on my own and find other ways to practise my languages.

Everyone is different and a method or an activity which works for someone may not be right for someone else. For example, perhaps it's too far from their optimal learning style or because they would find it boring or too stressful.

As a teacher, I really care about my students' progress and how they feel. I love languages and love helping people reach their goals and overcome their fears or whatever makes them feel stuck. I want a teacher who is very patient and who is not bored by the fact that at the beginning I speak at 'turtle speed'.

Anyone can improve if you give them a chance.

The teachers who speak for most of the lesson... are they aware that at most their students will become good listeners? How can students improve if they don't have the chance to speak? And not just by saying yes or no. If we want to become fluent, we have to speak. If it's a group class, talking to classmates is important. I agree, they will make mistakes, but we do not absorb what they say.

The other point is about correcting mistakes. Again, everyone is different and there are people who want to be corrected all the time. This may be useful when we have already reached a certain level of fluency and we don't make a mistake every five seconds, as is normal when we have just started. But especially at the beginning, what's the point of correcting every single word? No wonder everyone is afraid of speaking at the beginning!

What I think should always be corrected are mistakes that lead to miscommunication, for example words which offend or are shocking to hear, or things which make understanding impossible. For example, because we don't usually use subjects in Italian, verb endings are crucial, otherwise it would be impossible to understand or guess who is doing what. So, if someone wanted to say, 'I speak Italian' and instead of 'parlo italiano' they said 'parla italiano' (which means she/he speaks Italian), it might lead to confusion depending on the context. More interestingly, 'mi piace' (where the 'e' is pronounced as /e/) means 'I like'. But 'mi piaci' (where the second 'i' is pronounced as /i/) means 'I like you', which in Italian has a romantic connotation and it doesn't just mean 'I like you as a person'.

Then there are words and grammar points that aren't useful at a certain level: if a student is using the present tense where they should be using the subjunctive, what's the point in correcting them when they don't even know what the present and subjunctive tenses are used for?

The same goes for pronunciation. If bad pronunciation

of a word impedes understanding, it's better to correct it (although if everything is corrected at once, it's impossible to remember the correction and apply it), but for most students, correcting every little sound will just make them afraid of speaking. Our brain has to process sounds even before we're able to repeat them in our head, let alone while speaking.

We cannot learn and apply everything at once.

But I am not saying that students shouldn't be corrected. In fact, if we don't intervene when there's a recurring and serious mistake, these mistakes might fossilise and undoing them will be harder than not having made them in the first place. In most cases, it's enough to simply use a method that takes the student's current level into consideration as well as their personality.

And then there's fluency and accuracy. When we do grammar exercises, or when we say that we want others to correct every single mistake we make, we are focusing on accuracy.

When we speak (and make mistakes according to our current level), we are training fluency. Both are useful and how much we should focus on one or the other depends on our goal (speaking with friends, written exam, oral exam, etc).

What we often forget is that they are two different types of abilities and must be trained separately. Have you ever tried to learn something (a sport, for example) and your friend or instructor said so many things that you couldn't even remember them, let alone apply all of them at the same time? Concentrate on one goal/skill at a time. You will see more results if you switch between phases in which you concentrate on grammar topics and vocabulary (if possible, in an interactive and fun way) and sessions in which you just use what you know.

Apart from that, it's also important to me that the teacher is an interesting person to talk to and that they ask questions and keep the conversation going. Of course, as a student, I want to contribute to the conversation. It is important for students to be able to ask questions, because in real life we are not normally 'interviewed' when we talk to people – but in a lesson, and until I am fluent, I also need to be given the chance to talk because if I only ask questions, I won't be doing much of the talking.

A teacher doesn't have to change their natural way of speaking all the time (students still need authentic language), but they should know WHEN and IF to adapt their speaking speed, vocabulary and way of articulating sounds to make words clearer (especially for beginners).

The teacher's experience of communicating with foreigners in their mother tongue also helps because it improves their understanding of what students are trying to say – it's impossible to pronounce everything correctly, especially at the beginning.

In my experience, another important point is whether teachers have learnt foreign languages – even better if they themselves are still learning them as they can understand the students' struggles and can share their learning strategies.

Should you opt for a native speaker when looking for a teacher? Many people think so. I agree that the higher the level, the greater the advantage of working with a native speaker. However, the good thing about not being a native speaker is that, unless the person is exceptionally competent and has lots of experience, they will have gone through what you are going through and will know what is difficult.

This is particularly important for beginner levels. Plus, if they themselves have studied a certain language, they can usually explain things better and know where the traps are. If they speak many languages, they will also know the root of a certain mistake.

I never said that being a teacher was easy.

As with most jobs, vocation lies at the heart of successful language teaching. Being a teacher is a responsibility: you're helping people. Many students stop if they don't get on with their teacher (think of school and languages).

As my sister sometimes points out, you can find people who improvise as teachers because they need a job, as well as others who do it because it's what they love. For me, teaching languages is something I feel I was born to do. I deeply care about my students and always try to find new, interactive and innovative ways to teach them.

When I learn languages and I am looking for people to talk to for practice, if the other person is able to do all the above, it doesn't matter whether they have a language certificate or whether they can explain grammar to me. I learn language rules in books.

However, when I need to learn nuances or the difference between words and expressions, how often they are used, whether it's an important point etc., I can't expect my language partner to know all of that, and this is when I need a professional teacher or a language expert.

The core method

Now I would like to share with you the method I use as a language learner, which is the method I have used to learn all the languages I speak at an advanced level.

I have been learning and teaching languages for the past 20 years and my friends and students have often asked me how I managed to learn the 13 languages I teach and the several others I have studied.

Although everyone is different, there are certain learning strategies that work for just about everyone. I would like to share with you what I do when I want to study a new language or take it to the next level.

Understanding the most efficient way for each of us to learn languages is a job in itself. It's a sort of path of discovery. The best way to find out what works for you is to try out different strategies that interest and stimulate you. Feel free to try out a couple of things I share that interest you. At the same time, you should know that these things work amazingly well in combination – it's the combination of multiple factors that brings the most positive results, and every time my students, coachees or friends have applied the same method, it has worked really well.

I am always pleased when I can contribute my experience and passion for languages to help someone reach their goals and feel good about themselves! I haven't always felt good about my own learning so I love that I can help other people to with theirs. Knowing that something has helped you even in a small way would make me very happy.

Let's get started!

Strategy 1: Make sure that you practise the skill you want to improve.

What's clear when you are learning languages is that you must practise the skill you want to improve. For example, if your aim is to be able to speak a language within a short time, spending the whole time reading won't help you much when you want to talk. There are productive activities (speaking and writing), which help you produce the language and there are passive activities (listening and reading), which help you understand the language. Focus more on what is useful for you and for your goals.

A language is a system, so actually anything you learn is useful in the end. If you really enjoy reading, please keep doing it. Just remember to include some productive activities if your aim is to speak with people, otherwise you might get frustrated because you will understand a lot without being able to say much.

The same applies to multilingual learning, but there is a clear advantage: when studying similar languages, it will take you less effort to speak all of them. You really only have to train yourself not to mix them up at the beginning, and you can do so using the strategies I describe in different parts of this book. I have never had a student who needed more than two or three lessons to almost completely stop mixing up languages.

So, if your aim is to be able to talk to people, try to speak as much as possible from the very beginning. I know how challenging this is, but I also know that it's very rewarding. This is why I: a) only focus on very useful vocabulary and structures for my level and b) look for a very patient teacher (or person to talk to), who can put up with my extremely slow speaking speed.

The best way would be to study a bit every day and speak every day or every other day. Speaking a bit every week is the minimum required to keep you motivated and to see progress. How often you should speak depends on your goals.

Remember not to switch from your target language to English (or to your mother tongue if it's different to English) simply because it's easier. If your aim is speaking, only by speaking will you reach your goal. Of course, you can do other things between speaking sessions in order to feel more confident and be able to say more.

Strategy 2: Have fun with the language.

Another essential point is that you should have fun with the language. Each of us is unique and enjoys different things (or similar things in a different way or with a different goal). If you do things you enjoy, you are much more likely to keep doing them. The same applies to language learning.

If you use a book you don't enjoy or talk or read about things that don't interest you, or watch or listen to things you find boring, you are much more likely to stop doing them before you have learnt the language you wanted to learn so much.

Do what you love!

If you really enjoy singing, please sing! If you love reading, please do so. If you love series, watch them, and so on. Languages are systems, so each part of the language is connected to the others and each little thing that you learn will make sense in the end. As long as you don't expect to understand everything from the beginning, you can start having fun with the language right now!

Of course, some things are more suitable than others – it all depends on our level. However, a boring activity at the right level will not increase our chances of sticking to it. Nevertheless, activities that are higher than our level but that we find interesting can be beneficial if approached in the right way. For example, you can watch a series and the more episodes you watch, the more will you understand, or you can read a book you really wanted to read, look up very few words, and still be able to follow the story. You may not get all the nuances but page after page, you will understand more and more. Which leads me to my next tip: don't forget the benefits of passive learning.

Have you ever listened to something in a language and couldn't understand where a word started or finished? This is completely normal. Our brain has to a) get used to how words (and which words) are pronounced together, b) process rhythm and intonation, c) hear/distinguish the words we already know, and d) make sense of the other words that we don't know according to the context. All this can be improved with passive listening.

Another example: if you watch a series or read a book, there will be words which will be repeated many times (even when you don't know a certain word, you usually notice when it's repeated many times). The words that are repeated are important (either in general or in the context of your book or series). You can learn words just by paying attention to what you hear (even though at the beginning you can't understand much at all).

In the same way, you can revise/reinforce words you have already learnt in a much more useful way than just reading a list: words in context are the best for our memory because they will be linked to a situation and you will know when to use them.

When you listen to a large amount of content, your brain automatically starts to understand more. If you didn't understand much before, the first stage will be that you will start to distinguish where a word starts or ends. This is why if you learn a bit every day, you will start to see how your brain magically understands more and more.

Strategy 3: Listen to the language: the more input, the better.

This helps me: a) become familiar with the language and its sounds, b) revise words just by listening to them several times, c) understand in which contexts I can use the words I hear or study, d) understand which words are more frequently used in a language, e) activate my vocabulary and be able to speak with fewer hesitations and faster, and f) feel more confident when I speak or use certain words or expressions because I know they are correct.

Listening input can come from one or more activities, such as listening to different kinds of sources (radio, music, podcasts) or watching films, TV series and videos. Each of these activities can be very useful and has different advantages. I spend the largest proportion of my study time listening, as opposed to watching – ideally, I would spend 60% of my time studying on my own doing a listening activity, 30% speaking and 10% watching, because a) I can do it while I am doing something else, like working or studying and b) I can really train my ears and not rely on images to understand the meaning (this is why phone calls are much more difficult than face to face conversations, and if I train myself to understand only what I hear, watching a movie or talking to someone will seem like a piece of cake!).

Movies are great because it's easier to understand words in context through images. They are generally long, so you have the time to get used to the language, accents and situations and since there is only one plot line, important words are repeated. Podcasts are great because they are normally based on topics you are truly interested in or made by a person you like. TV series are also useful as words are repeated all the time because the situations don't change much between episodes.

I usually don't spend much time on 'active listening', that is, listening by trying to understand every single word. I only do 'active listening' for shorter periods of time, but frequently throughout the day. For example, I will be listening to the radio while working and, from time to time, I will need a short break, and this is when I will listen carefully to what is being said for a minute or two.

It's very effective, especially because the time you spent listening without paying much attention was still received and processed by your brain (it normally helps to start separating the flow of unintelligible sounds you hear into actual words even if you don't know their meaning). 'Passive listening' (listening while doing something else or listening in a relaxed way, as one's mental state affects how information is absorbed) helps in any case, provided you actually hear the voice, so only if the volume isn't too low.

On other occasions, I try to pay attention to all the words being said when I watch something – which I always do entirely in the target language and in most cases without subtitles, or with subtitles in the target language if I want to learn new words and expressions.

When a language is new, I prefer shorter sessions of 'active listening' combined with longer sessions of 'passive listening'.

In any case, whatever I choose to listen to will only be in the target language, even if I have zero understanding, or close to it, at the beginning – and I know that it won't be like that for long.

As I said, you need lots of input, but of course it must be fun – otherwise you are not likely to keep it up. You should be looking forward to it!

Strategy 4: Use different channels to see and hear words in different contexts.

It is very effective to use different channels. By using different channels (watching, listening, reading, writing), you will see words and structures in different contexts. This will help you a) remember things better (different stimuli, different senses), b) build connections between different things you learn, c) revise vocabulary and grammar structures just by being exposed to them, and d) learn (automatically/unconsciously) which words and structures can be used in a given context. Try out every channel and take the best from them!

When I listen to the radio, I listen to both music and conversations. Songs are more fun, and you can listen to them many times without getting bored. They are also great for learning pronunciation in an almost automatic way, if you sing along. However, there are some complications: a) words and word order are chosen by song writers, with the main purpose being to adapt to the music, so the lyrics often don't reflect how people speak and b) music normally makes it harder to understand a new language.

For this reason, I switch between songs and programmes in which people are talking. I prefer the news because although the speed is incredibly fast, it's great training. And, if you listen to it throughout the day, you will notice that topics are repeated, and you will hear the same or similar vocabulary again and again.

I also enjoy watching movies, especially if they reflect the culture of the language I am studying. Speaking a language also means being able to understand the culture. If we spoke well but didn't behave in an appropriate way according to the culture, it would be perceived as even more rude than behaving in a way unfamiliar to the culture while speaking the language poorly.

Apart from listening (or watching), which I find extremely useful and more interesting, I also read texts and books. I read something suitable for my level when I want to understand each word and the grammar behind it. I use these kinds of texts to revise the grammar I study by noticing cases, structures and the gender of words I have already studied. It can be a graduate-level reading book, an article or content found in textbooks.

I also read real books. I start doing this not long after I start studying a language, but I do NOT try to understand all the words. In fact, I almost never look words up and I start very slowly (just one or two sentences per evening at the beginning). And, above all, I am very kind to myself and I don't expect to understand much at the beginning.

The point of doing this (for me) is: a) to be able to see words in context, b) to be absorbed by a the story I really want to read (I always pick a book I am really interested in, always in the modern version of the language), c) to revise words I learn during the day (important words always come up over and over again), and d) to learn spelling without writing too much, and e) to get used to grasping the meaning from the context, without understanding all the words. Most adults struggle with this last point, and I think this is one of the biggest barriers to progressing and not getting frustrated. We simply cannot know all the words from the beginning and if we can live with that and just do our best, we won't get stuck in conversations.

If you combine this with daily study, you will see progress from the beginning: every day you will notice and understand words you didn't know the day before and this is very rewarding (and useful for revision). I only choose books I am really interested in, or books I have read in other languages (especially if the language is difficult for me).

More material is on the way, for example: podcasts in several languages which only include useful vocabulary for the level, combined with transcripts, vocabulary lists, grammar notes, flashcards and video courses in different languages as well as multilingual video courses.

Strategy 5: Always study with a textbook (or with reliable and structured material).

I always start with a good book because books are usually more reliable in terms of the information they contain, especially for grammatical accuracy. Of course, there are lots of great websites, but the information is often scattered across the site or there is information missing (perhaps because the website owner is still creating content).

At the beginning, I use a book to get an idea of what to expect in terms of grammar and I love when the information is structured so that I know how much and what I have ahead of me (in order to finish the book at least).

On the one hand I choose my book very carefully: it will accompany me at the very least for one month (normally longer). On the other hand, unless it's a fantastic book, I don't follow it 100%: I apply my method to it (I do what I know is useful and I skip what is less useful or what bores or frustrates me – your mental state is important).

On the contrary, when I study for a language exam, I also do the boring parts, just in my own way. Sometimes I use exams as a trigger to learn a language in a more in-depth way. The choice of book is very important to me because a) I want to use my time efficiently, b) I want to see results, and c) I want to keep motivated and looking forward to using the material I have chosen.

When learning my languages, I used many textbooks.

I enjoyed a lot of them, though not necessarily all the content. Something was often missing: too much theory compared to practice, the examples were words I would never use in real life – or if they could have been useful at some point or in a certain situation, they were not useful for conversations, the audio was too slow/quick, there was no audio at all or there was too little/much information.

For some languages, it is possible to find lots of material, some very helpful and some less helpful. But for others, the very traditional way in which languages are taught – which either doesn't work for the majority of people (how many people do you know who learnt languages well at school?) or is too slow (you will start speaking and using the languages after several semesters, e.g. I have seen university courses in which you need a whole semester to learn the alphabet!!!) – hinders the students' progress.

I believe it's possible to have fun and effective classes from the beginning.

For this reason, I give workshops where I not only teach more than one language at the same time, but also 'difficult languages', so that we can see that it IS possible to speak any language from the beginning (what we are able to say depends on the language and what we find difficult). Participants start speaking after just a few minutes, even when learning languages like Russian, Hindi or Greek.

When learning some languages, I used a selection of different of books because I couldn't get everything I needed from just one, and they weren't particularly interesting. This is why I created my own learning material and courses. I love making what many people say is complicated easy, and I do want people to speak from the very beginning and see that they can a) learn anything and b) use it and remember it.

How do you find the right book for you?

This is what I normally do: according to where I am living, I look for the book: a) on the internet (if I haven't heard of the book, I read the index and, if possible, I choose the 'look inside' option, that allows you to preview some of its pages), b) in a regular book shop (but the choice is limited and not necessarily the best), c) in a specialised book shop (I don't have one near me so I try to look for one when I travel), d) by asking friends to have a look in one near where they live or asking friends to suggest one and asking them why they like it, or e) by asking friends who I think enjoy similar things to me, when it comes to languages.

How to recognise a good textbook

The first thing I do is see what kind of vocabulary it offers. Do I recognise words I actually use in my everyday life? Does it contain several words I never use because they relate to situations in which I would not normally use the language? For example: when I learn a language, what I want is to connect with people. For this, I need words and language structures that enable me to start having a conversation from the beginning.

Many books start with numbers, directions, food names,

hotel room bookings, ordering things in a restaurant etc. These things may come in handy at some point, but how can I have a conversation with that vocabulary? It's practically impossible.

I have travelled a lot – maybe you have too – and in my experience, as long as you pay, you will be fed! Most restaurants have menus in English, and in Asia, you usually find pictures of the food too. And if the problem is that you want to explain what you can't or don't eat, this isn't something taught in books anyway.

In my opinion, at the beginning of our language learning journey, we mostly need expressions such as 'I would like' (or the equivalent when ordering something), 'without' together with some foods you never eat (especially for languages with cases, because the noun normally change its ending), 'I'm allergic to' together with the food item you can't eat, 'thank you' and 'please' (or the equivalent) – plus some of the foods you usually order (not necessarily the plate name as it may not exist, but the main ingredient). Maybe you would need the word for 'bill', but I doubt they would let you go without paying…!

In a supermarket, we normally just pick up things and take them to the till, without the need for speaking. What's more, useful and culture-specific expressions, such as what the cashier says to you, are not taught in books. If you need to talk to someone at the counter, you can learn phrases such as 'I would like', plus the things you might buy, such as cheese, meat or fish. In most cases, you can simply point at something or say 'this'/'that'.

I'm not saying that it's necessary to be able to say everything we want to say. On the contrary, I dislike the feeling of not being able to say what I need in order to communicate, and that's why the further I progress in a language, the more I learn less-frequently used things. However, we have to start somewhere and can't learn everything at once, so to keep myself motivated, I start with the things which bring me most joy, like talking to people, getting to know other mentalities and making new friends.

It all comes down to what YOU will use more often and what your goal is. I know so many people who learn pre-compiled word lists through apps. In theory, these apps are for beginners but they contain words which are not useful for conversations. How can I use a list of fruit list conversations? Even if I loved to talk about healthy eating, it's not really a topic for beginners and words without language structures that help us create sentences and talk about the subject are just useless.

Another topic which I avoid at the very beginning is 'asking for directions'. How often do you really ask for directions? Nowadays with online (and offline) maps or apps, I rarely do so. And even if I was in a country without access to such a map, would I understand the answer?! The replies I get won't correspond with what is taught in my textbook, which will only include a few words on the topic, and the people I ask won't know what I have studied and what is easy or difficult for me to understand.

In the beginning (after a few weeks of learning), I just learn the three most useful words on this topic: 'right', 'left' and 'straight ahead', avoiding more complicated terms, such as 'cross the road', 'turn', 'pass', 'next to', etc. On the contrary, words like 'where', 'when', 'what', 'at' ('what time'), etc. are terms I learn as soon as possible. More information on useful words can be found in 'Strategy 7'.

Because I know how difficult it can be to find good textbooks and even more to find good material to combine them with, I wrote single-language and multilingual online courses based on all the language learning strategies I discuss in this book. These courses include interactive PDFs as textbooks in which I only use very useful vocabulary and language structures (according to the level), with embedded audios (for example, with me asking questions or answering them etc.), interactive quizzes, pronunciation insights, videos in which I explain grammar (related to one language or comparing languages in an easy and fun way to help you optimise your learning process), podcasts, flashcards with only the useful words for the level, and much more.

The second thing I pay attention to when choosing a textbook is which language structures are taught and whether they are a) useful, b) well-structured in terms of charts/tables/summaries, and c) whether they are highlighted, easy to find and be reviewed. Language structures are what really allow us to speak. I can know thousands of words, but if I can't put them into sentences, how can I be understood?

And the third thing I do is try to find textbooks that present a clear explanation of verb forms, especially of past and future tenses (or the language's way of expressing the equivalent), which is what people mostly talk about. More on this very important point can be found in 'Strategy 8'.

And last but not least, I prefer books with audio – especially if I'm a beginner. For higher levels, audio isn't absolutely necessary. Sometimes if I can't find a good textbook, I'll settle for a grammar book that is structured in a communicative way (with many examples of daily usage of the language[s]).

Multilingual material

If you are studying (or want to study) multiple languages at the same time, and depending of the languages you want to study, it can seem impossible to find good multilingual material. There are very good books for comparing languages, but they aren't textbooks, therefore you must be very motivated to read them from A to Z. I read some of them and I loved them, but they are not suited to beginners as they are mostly grammar-oriented – this may be good or bad thing, it depends on your previous experience with grammar (some people love it and others hate it).

Single-language textbooks that are each published for different language are NOT designed for multilingual learning. First of all, they don't offer language comparisons or explanations of language features.

Secondly, most of them are just a copy of another. I believe that books for different languages shouldn't have the same structure. I understand the business reasons behind it: you produce a book once, duplicate it, and apply the same pattern to all of them. This is very convenient from a business point of view, but I believe that the books should be much more language-specific than they normally are. I am a multiple language learner myself and I personally find it extremely boring to read the same material over and over again in different languages.

Something similar happens with podcasts, flashcards and books geared towards learning different languages through stories. How could I be happy and stay motivated when reading the exact same thing more than once?

And above all, what is important in one language might not be so important in another language or it may have a different degree of difficulty. I personally teach and write my material according to what is really important when starting to speak or use a language and to the true degree of frequency and usefulness.

Sometimes it can be useful to read your favourite book in other languages, but books have hundreds of pages, and so you don't get the impression that you are going through the same material over and over again. The fact that you have already read a certain book helps you understand the content more easily when you read it in a language you know to a lesser degree. More importantly, you are very motivated because you know you love that book and it makes you happy to read it again AND in another language.

I don't look up every word when reading stories. I let myself be absorbed by the story and by the words, and important words will come up more and more often. This is why combining activities is so important: if you keep studying, you will find the same words you learn in your books.

Studying with material which is not IDENTICAL across all languages helps me keep languages separate in my brain. If books had the same identical content across different languages, I would have difficulty remembering where I read something, and I might start confusing language features or certain words.

For example, in my courses, no single-language course is a copy of another and even in my multilingual courses, no single-language parts are identical because the material is presented according to what is most relevant to a certain language.

Resources: I know how difficult it can be to find good learning material. This is why I've dedicated time to providing my students with a list of resources according to the language or languages they are studying. It could be music, videos, podcasts, books, textbooks, etc.

Strategy 6: Always set a daily goal when using a textbook.

This goal could be to get through a certain number of pages (or just one page according to the book, my time and my goal) or a set amount of time. A certain number of pages is my favourite because: a) I know in advance how long it will take me to finish the book, b) it gives me a vision: I can visualise when I am likely to have learnt the book's content – even if I don't know everything, I will definitely have an idea of the language and I will know more than before (a feasible goal with definite results), and c) being able to grasp the book in my hands and see the progress I am making helps motivate me and gives me hope.

The important thing is not to set too high a goal: mentally, it's much better to say less and do more if we have more time than see how we have fallen short of what we promised to do.

Setting myself a fixed amount of time is useful when I really only have a certain amount of time that I can dedicate to learning each day, or when I study more than one language at the same time. The most important part of setting time is not to have distractions: 5 to 30 minutes a day can be enough providing we really are studying and not looking at our phone etc.

Strategy 7: Focus on useful words.

Focus on useful words, especially connectors and words in your area of interest. The higher your level, the better it is to read about other topics as well. However, in most cases, you will end up talking about what interests you or about things related to your job (which hopefully is in your area of interest!)

Useful words are also words everyone needs, such as adverbs and connectors. I use or at least I write word lists especially for exams. Your passive vocabulary must be more substantial than active vocabulary, in order to understand and react. Let's take a look at this in more detail!

Learn specific words: there are words I know I will always use and need. Normally we either talk about the past or the future, so I need words like 'yesterday', 'last month' or 'next year' (time adverbs). We also talk about our habits (especially when we talk about our hobbies or work, and when we want to arrange to meet up), so I need frequency adverbs like 'from time to time', 'sometimes', 'often' or 'never'.

I also need linking words (connectors). At a beginner level, we mostly use words like 'but', 'and' and 'because', but as soon I want to express myself and convey a more specific meaning, I start needing words like 'although', 'however', 'since', 'as', etc.

I also need words which are related to what I could talk about (e.g. sport, travels, siblings, my daily routine, appointments), question words (how, why, how long, etc.). With these types of words, together with useful verbs and structures, you will already be able to say so much!

Let's see what structures are: structures are combination of words and verbs that just by changing one or two words around can help you say a lot. For example: 'How do you say...', 'How do you write...', 'How do you pronounce...', etc.

Learning specific structures: I know I will need structures such as 'I have' and 'I am'. I also know that I often use structures like 'If I had time I would' or 'I would like' etc. They may seem intimidating, but it is actually the same pattern repeated, so I will end up learning them, but not on my first day of course.

Structures are great because if I know a certain structure, but I am missing a word, I can always look it up, which is very easy. Whereas, looking up a structure is not obvious, and I cannot be sure that the result I get from an online translator is really what I was looking for, as machine translation is not yet smart enough for some word combinations (especially in certain languages).

At the beginning, I concentrate only on very useful vocabulary, which is what I want to actively remember. I also need passive vocabulary, words that I understand but that I would not use myself, because I need to understand people when they use a different construction or when they talk about hobbies different from mine.

Because I don't like learning words by heart, I learn them in context through listening and reading.

What I really try to avoid at the beginning, if I can, are many of the typical 'touristic' sentences like 'Turn right' or 'Can I have the menu?'. Honestly, in most countries, these kinds of things are easy to overcome with the help of Google Maps or just by speaking English (if I am asking how to get somewhere, I know that I won't have a meaningful conversation and that I most likely need that information as soon as possible). I always learn a language to be able to talk to people and have meaningful conversations and this is what I study and teach.

When I can already speak a language a bit, of course I'll learn other things too, but if my aim is to interact with people and have meaningful conversations, then I start by learning something which can really help me have a conversation. If my aim is to travel to a different country, spend time mainly with my partner and friends, and just be able to get by in restaurants, then on the contrary, it is the right vocabulary to learn.

Strategy 8: Focus only on useful verbs and structures.

What is useful depends on your level (and on your goal): tenses, especially past and future tenses, or the equivalent in a language (some languages use the present tense to express the meaning of a future action) are used all the time because we usually talk about something we (or someone else) did or are about to do. Of course we talk about other things too but, if you paid attention to conversations around you for a week or so, you would definitely notice that this is what people talk the most about.

I never learn words by heart, although I do make my own lists. But I learn them by using them (in conversation or by building sentences) and especially by finding them again in context (texts, radio or audio).

When it comes to exams, I try to learn all the verb forms, but I don't spend hours trying to memorise them. At the beginning, (A1-A2) I only choose verbs I know I will use – this is why I make my list. I don't need verbs like 'abdicate' (which I have actually found in verb lists, or as examples of a certain pronunciation feature) or other not-so-common words I find in word lists or in pronunciation tables. Rather, I need useful verbs like: 'to drink', 'to sleep', 'to play', 'to say, 'to tell', 'to buy', 'to sell', 'to study', 'to learn', etc.

I always need modal verbs like 'to have to', 'must', 'want' and 'can', because they allow me to express my feelings and thoughts.

I always create a list of all the useful verbs, according to the level, but if the language is difficult at the beginning, I concentrate on the first and second persons and the formal way to address people.

It does not mean that I will not learn them later on, but first I focus on what I and others use most frequently. At the beginning, I can also avoid saying 'we went' by saying 'I went to the cinema with my friend'.

Strategy 9: Work in a different way with things like cases, exceptions, conjugation tables and word lists.

At the beginning, I learn exceptions only for things that I know I will need on a regular basis, such as recurrent words or verbs for my level and for the situation I am going to use the language(s) in.

What's the point of learning exceptions NOW if they apply to words that I will use, if at all, once I've reached an advanced level of the language?

I do study conjugation tables, but I do this for exams and, in general, I try to learn them by using them (the more I see I need them – for example, if I notice that I often need a certain word when I speak, I will more concentrate on that) and revising them by listening to them.

I always focus more on verbs and language structures (rather than words) because they are by far the most important elements in a language: you can look up words, but in order to use a verb correctly, you have to know how the language works.

The same is true for cases, but not all cases are of equal importance: accusative and dative cases are normally the most important and recurrent ones, so I concentrate more on them. Cases are not of equal importance in all languages and they are not always referred to using the word 'case'. For instance, in Italian and Spanish there are no 'cases', but there are essentially pronouns which have the same function (e.g. 'la'/'gli' in Italian and 'la'/'le' in Spanish). I learn cases by starting with the most useful first.

I only use flashcards if they are reliable. I don't usually write my own because it takes too much time. Instead, I normally learn words in context and by using and listening to the language. But if I had word lists with words I really use (and was sure about the reliability), I would use them: this is why I have created them for my students according to my experience of what is useful at any level.

Strategy 10: Adjust the method to your learning

style and concentrate on what matters to you.

Build your own learning method, taking into account important factors: a) focus (focus on what matters to you, in terms of useful vocabulary and structures, interesting material and activities, skills you want to improve), b) input (regular and from different channels), c) quality time (quality time could mean spending just five minutes doing the things you find most helpful, and with no distractions), and d) mental state (embrace learning, have fun with the language, be kind to yourself); goal setting (create your vision, set your goals and define small steps to follow).

Focusing on the right things will help you make quicker progress, enable you to look back with satisfaction at all you have learnt and keep you highly motivated.

Unless your level is already advanced, you don't need to learn all the words, structures and expressions you find in books or textbooks. You need words that are useful to you and that help you talk about your life, because this is normally what we talk about when we meet people.

Strategy 11: Study the language(s) you want to learn for five minutes a day.

Most people stay motivated by seeing results. Study each language you want to learn for just five minutes a day and you can be sure that you are moving forward and that today you will be at least one step closer to your final goal.

Do it before your busy day starts, then it's done, and you don't have to think about it until the next day. If later you see that you have more time, reward yourself with a language activity you really enjoy. Don't wait for the perfect moment (or period of your life), or you'll be waiting forever. No one has time but we can MAKE time for what matters to us. And if it's only five minutes, anyone can do it!

Start today, the rest will come.

Many people talk badly about themselves and if you listen carefully, you will often hear 'I can't'. This is normal as we are often pushed by society to be top performers. But in order to get there, we have to learn. This is often forgotten, and so when we aren't satisfied with our performance, we say to ourselves: 'I have such bad pronunciation', 'I can't pronounce anything correctly', 'I don't know anything', 'It's too difficult', 'I am too old', and so on.

A stress-free mental state is important for absorbing information – this is why you should focus on what you ARE doing and what you CAN do in those five minutes, rather than what you don't know. What we don't know yet isn't important now. What we DO now will help us reach our goals.

Before it becomes a part of your routine, starting your study session can be difficult at first. But if you decide on the time and place, and have everything ready to start studying, you will already have removed the biggest challenges faced by those who want to start a new routine.

To give you an example, when you are on a diet or have decided not to eat or drink something but you don't plan your alternatives in advance, then the day you arrive home hungry (or frustrated), you will open your fridge and...voilà! If instead you buy the food you want to eat, it's already there waiting for you at home and it will be easier to stick to the plan. The same happens with any new habit: if you have your learning material prepared and a clear idea of how to use it and have decided on the time and place, you just need to sit down and get started.

There are many things that you can do in those five minutes. The most important thing is to use them in an effective way.

If I only had five minutes, I would choose something that allowed me to learn or be exposed to very useful words, language structures and verbs. I would read or listen to these words, structures and verbs in context (this is possible if you have carefully and in advance chosen the learning material you want to work on according to the many tips I gave you in other sections of this book). The other thing I do is revise self-made lists of these words, structures and verbs that I created in my previous study sessions (either from studying in the past or from what I studied recently, our brain will retain the information more quickly, so even if I don't actively remember the information, some parts of my brain do).

Please don't use precompiled wordlists with words you don't use every day (if you don't want to write your own, at least remove the words that you don't normally use and concentrate on what matters to you and what helps you express your thoughts).

Some ideas: listen to something already prepared/ chosen. The most efficient thing to do would be to prepare for more than one session in one go, e.g. a certain number of podcasts or videos you enjoy, a playlist (and maybe the lyrics) of the songs you want to listen to, a bookmark on your computer or phone with the radio station you want to listen to etc. Don't forget to listen to things like the news or radio programmes in which people just talk – music is more enjoyable, and it is great to train pronunciation, but the lyrics don't always reflect everyday conversations or correct grammar!

Note: you will soon be able to find carefully-chosen vocabulary, verbs and structure lists combined with podcasts and other material on my website.

Even if I don't have much time, I train different skills using different channels because everything serves a purpose and has its benefits. In other parts of my book, I talked about active and passive listening, different types of reading, such as extensive reading without looking for words especially with books, shorter texts suited to your level while looking up words, and 'observer reading', where you notice and focus on how the rules you already know are applied to the text you are reading – this is very helpful when studying languages with cases as it helps you notice forms without having to study them by heart.

Train the skill you want to be good at.

It seems obvious, but I have spoken to so many people who say they are frustrated because they study a lot but can't speak. Then when I ask them how often they speak; the answer is almost always 'never'. It's like wanting to drive a car just by knowing the theory. You have to apply what you learn. If your aim is listening or reading, you can improve just by studying your minimum of five minutes a day in an efficient way.

If you want to be able to speak, on the top of your study routine, you should talk to people. With whom and how often will depend on many factors (where you live, lifestyle etc.), but try to speak at least once a week. There are many ways to learn that don't require much time or money (e.g. a language group exchange or a person you can have a live/remote language exchange with). Depending on several factors, it may take you a while to get it set up, but once it is set up, you're ready to go!

Once you start, remember: your mental state is important, so don't judge yourself. Find someone who has more or less the same level as you (unless you prefer to work with a teacher) so that you can both speak without worrying about your speed and mistakes. Talking to native speakers is great, but unless your level is already quite good, it could be quite stressful because it takes us much longer to build our sentences and express everything we want to say at the beginning.

Another important thing to remember when we start speaking a new language is that we have to train and learn how to simplify what we want to say: it's impossible to be able to speak at an advanced level from the very beginning. Try to simplify your message, as if you were talking to a child. For example, you could prepare a short description of yourself to overcome the stress of speaking a language for the first time. Having something ready will help make you feel more at ease.

I personally don't enjoy learning things by heart but I must admit that the one time I wrote a short script of what I wanted to say to someone I had just met, it really helped me a) be aware of what kinds of things I could say or talk about, b) have at least an idea of how I could say those things (for example, what structures I needed or could use to say something).

Another very important point in my opinion is that many people are not aware that when they are not understood while speaking a foreign language, it's usually not because they made a mistake but rather because they didn't finish their sentence.

In a way, it's as if the fear of making mistakes blinds them from seeing that no one would understand them in their native language if they didn't finish their sentences. When I see students or other people who do that, I want to hug them and say, 'don't worry!', 'I WILL understand you' – I just don't read minds.

I often understand what people want to say before they finish their sentences because I have talked to thousands of people in different languages and I often know what people might say. However, there are cases when it's just impossible to guess, not because of mistakes but because there are no words. When you have spoken to foreigners, did they say everything correctly? I'm sure they didn't. Could you understand what they wanted to say or at least the main idea? I guess most of the time. I am not talking about single words, but rather a conversation. Likewise, I am talking about cases in which the problem is not grammar but pronunciation. Pronunciation does not have to be perfect for you to be understood.

The most important thing is for the letters to be pronounced correctly, especially at the beginning of words, because this is what our brain processes the most when trying to understand the meaning of what we hear.

People often forget that the reason we speak in a real-life

situation is to communicate. Even when our goal is fluency, it is not possible to reach fluency THROUGH fluency. We have to pass through a phase where we, just like everyone else, make mistakes. Mistakes are good! It means that we are trying!

Concentrate on the communication itself and relax as much as you can because when we are stressed, we simply cannot perform well because our brains are too busy with other thoughts. If you think: 'I will learn...I AM learning and I am trying...there is no need to get stressed, I am getting there, just relax and enjoy the conversation', you will see that your ability to speak will improve a lot.

If you have not done so yet, read the section 'With or without a teacher?'

Study each language you want to learn for at least 5 minutes before you go to work (or to university) to make sure that you have worked on your goals that day. If during the day you have more time, study a bit more. Of course, 10 to 30 minutes per language would be ideal but not many people have that time, so do a minimum of five minutes as soon as possible during the day, and anything on top of that is a bonus.

Of course, if you have a date by which you need to be able to speak a certain language, things are different: count the days (or hours) you have available, choose the material or activities you want to learn and make sure to dedicate enough time to the activities in order to achieve your goal. For example, take a good book and divide the number of pages you have by the number of days you have to study.

You will find more practical advice on this in Strategy 12.

Strategy 12: Build your routine.

I discussed the importance of routine in detail in Part 4, but here I would like to focus on the practical part of it.

Motivation is what makes us start but habit is what keeps the ball rolling. Even people who hate routine perform most of their daily actions because of a routine and in an almost automatic way: eating at a certain time, taking a shower, brushing their teeth, talking while driving, taking the same route to work, etc.

When you build your routine, even if something seemed difficult at the beginning, after just a few days you will be doing it automatically with almost no effort at all. And, the longer you stick to your habit, the more your brain will be craving it.

Build your routine for language learning: decide on a time when you will study your language, no matter what. Choose a time when you are the least likely to be interrupted. Choose a doable amount of time to start with: 5 minutes will do! If we are motivated, finding five minutes a day is always possible!

This can be your core learning: if you stick to it, you will improve no matter what. Stick to your routine: same time (hour) and same minimum amount of time. Everything else is a bonus.

Best time to study

Many people wonder what the best time of day to study is. In reality, there is no 'best time' as everyone is different. Personally, my favourite time to study has changed a lot over the years. When I was a teenager, I loved studying in the evenings when it was dark, and I had no distractions. Nowadays, I prefer to do creative and learning activities in the morning.

Not everyone is a morning person and I am not one by nature. But I do see the huge benefits of doing what matters to me first thing in the morning. I know that for most people, this seems impossible: we have to get to work or school or go to a lecture, and many of us have kids. But if you have ever tried to diet, you will know that if you start your day without doing something you planned on in order to get you closer to your goal and you start going in the opposite direction (for example, starting the day by allowing yourself exceptions to the plan), it won't get better as the day progresses. On the contrary, if you stick to your plan during the first part of the day, you will be inclined to keep it up throughout the day.

The good news is that learning languages is much easier than dieting because if you learn during the first part of your day without making any additional effort to get you closer to your goal on that day, you won't mess anything up.

Do the minimum amount in the morning and if you don't want to do more, you can still be proud of what you have already done. If you want to do more, you can consider it a bonus and instead of feeling the pressure, you can enjoy knowing that everything on the top of what you have already done will simply help you more.

When you diet, evening time is when it's most difficult to stick to your plan. The same thing applies to any other goal that requires willpower. This is because your mind is packed full of things that have happened during the day (good things, bad things, worries, things that you still have to do, things that you couldn't finish or even begin), and we normally feel tired or less energetic. Most people find it very difficult to concentrate in the evening.

Actually, what normally happens is that if we are already used to doing something, we can do it even in less-than-convenient circumstances, at any time of the day. For example, most of us can work (or study) late in the evening or at night if necessary, because we are used to this type of activity. But when it comes to things outside of our daily routine, it's harder to keep focused and above all, it's difficult to get started. This is why it is very important to maintain a routine: the more often we do something (even just for 10 minutes), the easier it will get.

And once the day has started, unless you are extremely organised and disciplined and can shut everything out until you reach your goal for the day, unexpected things always come up. And once you start procrastinating, it's very likely that you will stop doing so until you absolutely have to (which isn't normally enforced unless you are studying languages at school). Your goal will move further and further away, and you will experience a decline in motivation, as results normally motivate us and the lack of results make us abandon projects.

But it doesn't have to be this way. Learn a bit every day, even if it's just for five minutes, and you will always be moving forward, which is what matters in the end.

If, on the contrary, you are a night owl and you find it productive to study in the evening, this can also work. But if you have already tried and something always comes up and you don't learn, then why not try something in the morning and see the amazing effects on your efficiency, progress and mood?

The best time of the day to study is a time that we know we can commit to, in order to fit it into our daily routine so that it becomes a habit.

N.B. if you haven't ever gone on a diet, you can think of anything else you wanted to learn that required effort and willpower.

Possible study routines

Now I would like to suggest two effective study routines. Their effectiveness will depend on your current learning goal:

For those of you who don't have a specific deadline but want to move forward and be closer to their goals every day:

1) Study each language you want to learn for 5 to 10 minutes every day.

- The time must be used wisely (this book discusses both the materials you could use and the activities you could do)

- No distractions

- Study at the same time every day to build a routine

- Choose a time you know you can commit to

2) Speak these languages at least once a week.

- Don't worry about making mistakes. Mistakes are the way to success. A quote I love states: "If you are not failing, it's because you are not trying hard enough."

- Speak for at least 30 minutes

If you are a beginner, speak:

a) with a teacher or tutor who lets you speak for the majority of the time even if you cannot speak at all! There are MANY ways to help beginners speak from the first moment and I use them all the time when I teach. If you want to learn multiple languages at the same time, consider multilingual lessons too. The big advantage is that you can train all your languages in one session and you learn how not to mix them up. For example, my students train up to 3 languages in a 60-minute session and up to 6 languages in a 90-minute session, and after two or three sessions, they almost never mix languages up.

b) with a language partner (in person or online) who is willing to split up the time equally (for example, 30 minutes in your target language and 30 minutes in their target language) and do NOT switch to another language you know. This could be a bit challenging at the beginning but is very rewarding in the end. Sometimes we are convinced we can't speak or don't know enough. Maybe we don't know enough to say something interesting (this is why we are speaking to a language partner or a teacher and not to someone we want to be hired by), but we certainly know enough to say and train what we already know! Even if it's just a combination of random words or introducing ourselves. After we have trained what we know, we can learn something new (of course, if you're not a real beginner, you can start directly with something new because you will automatically use the things you already know in a conversation).

Note: you will soon be able to find useful material for the most effective language exchange on my website and if you subscribe, you will be notified.

And don't forget that even when we can't say many interesting things, we can still show our personality (most of our communication is not verbal anyway) and connect with people! To do this, we need an in-person exchange or if online, then with video.

c) to different people at a group language exchange (same rules as above, although dividing the time equally can be a bit challenging according to the type of event you go to).

d) with people who are learning the same language as you are. The advantage is that you don't feel judged and you can both enjoy talking to each other despite the speed and the mistakes because it's a win-win situation for both of you. Some people just want to speak to native speakers but unless your level is already good or if you have really good and extremely patient foreign friends, it's not very realistic to expect them to talk to you for hours without an exchange.

e) with your foreign friends: if you are a beginner, my advice is to ask here and there how to say something in their language and try to use it when a similar discussion comes up. In this way, you can learn real-life expressions. If your level is higher (and they agree!), you can also just talk to them during activities you do together (or do an exchange).

f) If you are living abroad in the country of your target language, try one or more of the following things: talk to people whenever possible (and appropriate) and do activities you enjoy that are taught or carried out in your target language (dance classes, hiking, sports etc.). In this way, you will meet people and be exposed to the language. If people switch to English all the time, don't be discouraged, remember that you are entitled to speak the language you want, as are they.

3) Listen to the language as much as you can: don't forget the benefits of both active and passive learning so you can listen to anything you want while doing other things, such as working, studying, driving and commuting, and it will work! If you have time, watch something, in the evening for instance, when you are too tired to study or do anything else. Be kind to yourself and ENJOY what you are watching: relax and let yourself be absorbed by the story. I personally find that watching without subtitles is much more effective in the long term, but if you do want subtitles, then select them in the target language.

For those who want to see results as soon as possible:

Do as suggested above, but on the top of that:

4) Add more time to your daily studying routine (for example, go from 30 minutes to 1 hour).

5) During your lunch break (or any break during the day), do something you enjoy. For example, I enjoy walking during my break, and I do one of the following activities: listening to music, listening to language audio files, talking to friends (if possible, in another language) or having a speaking practice session while walking. If you want to sit, you could read something, study a bit more, watch something, etc.

6) Use flashcards (by using apps or real cards), but only very useful words and structures. When I am serious about a language, I also create my own word list, because it contains words I know I really need and use – it's not random a word list with words I will never really use.

7) If you enjoy writing, and especially if you don't get to speak often, write something in your target language(s). It doesn't have to be long – anything will do. It can be something about your day (maybe in a simplified way), a message (or an imaginary message) to a friend or, if your level is a bit higher, a short story.

A final tip: write down the learning activities you enjoy the most and spend some time finding the right material. This is worth doing because once you start looking for something, you will find many more things and you won't have to look for new material for a long time (if at all!).

To make it easier for you, I made a list of possible language learning activities. You will find this list in the appendix.

Conclusion

The aim of this book is to discuss the advantages of multilingual learning and provide you with an efficient multilingual method (which can also partially be used for single-language learning), language learning strategies, and a variety of language learning activities, study routines and multilingual and coaching advice and tools.

I really hope that you have found some inspiration and guidance in what you have read.

If you are considering learning multiple languages at the same time, I hope this book has encouraged you to start your language learning journey.

If you were already learning more than one language at the same time, I hope this book has given you some useful insights and tips to help you along the way.

If you were just in need of a little motivation, I hope this book has served as a small reminder of everything you are capable of.

To all you budding polyglots out there, I salute you!

Appendix

Appendix I: Goal setting with my Language learning planner

I really want you to succeed. Use my Language learning planner to set your daily and long-term goals and to keep track of your achievements.

Most importantly, it also contains motivational tips to accompany you on your language learning journey. And last but not least, its retrospective questions are a powerful tool to help you improve your routine straight away.

To download my Language learning planner as an interactive PDF, visit the webpage:
https://speakfromdayonewithelisa.us20.list-manage.com/subscribe?u=20a558cff7e8157a54a59684c&id=fa573f4342

Appendix II: Language learning activity list

Here is a list of activities you could consider doing in your spare time.

Whenever you have some time to dedicate to language learning, have a look at this list and choose what you are going to do.

Feel free to add your own activities to the list.

Bonus tip: Print this page and write the exact names of the books, podcast channels (and, if possible, the episode numbers), series and movies names you could use next to each activity.

Having something prepared will help you avoid wasting time. It takes a bit of time at the beginning but remember, it all goes towards optimising your language learning. For example, when you have only five minutes, you can start learning directly and won't waste those five minutes on deciding what to do.

- Listening to a podcast
- Watching a series
- Reading an article
- Listening to music
- Writing (or sending an audio message) to friends in your favourite language (even if you don't usually communicate in that language)

- Listening to the radio (news or music)
- Reading a page of your textbook or grammar book
- Reading a novel
- Revising one or two notes from a lesson (only relevant words, verbs, expressions or language structures please!)
- Using an app to learn languages (don't make it your only learning activity, depending on the app, it may be a helpful complementary activity but it is rarely enough to make huge progress)
- Singing songs/reading the lyrics
- Watching an interesting video on YouTube
- Watching a movie or a part of it (best without subtitles or with subtitles in the target language)

Appendix III: Study routines

I've summarised the effective study routines described in Part 5 in a practical way to give you a handy overview of what you could do to reach your current learning goal:

For those of you who don't have a specific deadline but want to move forward and be closer to your goals every day:

1) Study each language you want to learn for 5 to 10 minutes every day.

- The time must be used wisely (refer to Part 4 and 5 as well as Appendix II to decide on the activities you will focus on)
- No distractions
- Study at the same time every day to build a routine
- Choose a time you know you can commit to

2) Speak these languages at least once a week.

- Don't worry about making mistakes. Mistakes are the way to success
- Speak for at least 30 minutes

3) Listen to the language as much as you can: don't forget the benefits of both active and passive learning so you can listen to anything you want while doing other things, such as working, studying, driving and commuting, and

it will work! If you have time, watch something, in the evening for instance, when you are too tired to study or do anything else. Be kind to yourself and ENJOY what you are watching: relax and let yourself be absorbed by the story. I personally find that watching without subtitles is much more effective in the long term, but if you do want subtitles, then select them in the target language.

For those who want to see results as soon as possible:

1) Study each language you want to learn for at least 30 minutes every day (choose the exact amount of time according to your goal and deadline but set a feasible daily goal to make sure you stick to it).

- The time must be used wisely (refer to Part 4 and 5 as well as Appendix II to decide on the activities you will focus on)
- No distractions
- Study at the same time every day to build a routine
- Choose a time you know you can commit to

2) Speak these languages at least once a week.
- Don't worry about making mistakes. Mistakes are the way to success
- Speak for at least 30 minutes

3) Listen to the language as much as you can: don't forget the benefits of both active and passive learning so you can listen to anything you want while doing other things,

such as working, studying, driving and commuting, and it will work! If you have time, watch something, in the evening for instance, when you are too tired to study or do anything else. Be kind to yourself and ENJOY what you are watching: relax and let yourself be absorbed by the story. I personally find that watching without subtitles is much more effective in the long term, but if you do want subtitles, then select them in the target language.

4) During your lunch break (or any break during the day), do something you enjoy. For example, I enjoy walking during my break, and I do one of the following activities: listening to music, listening to language audio files, talking to friends (if possible, in another language) or having a speaking practice session while walking. If you want to sit, you could read something, study a bit more, watch something, etc.

5) Use flashcards (by using apps or real cards), but only very useful words and structures. When I am serious about a language, I also create my own word list, because it contains words I know I really need and use – it's not random a word list with words I will never really use.

6) If you enjoy writing, and especially if you don't get to speak often, write something in your target language(s). It doesn't have to be long – anything will do. It can be something about your day (maybe in a simplified way), a message (or an imaginary message) to a friend or, if your level is a bit higher, a short story.

By the same author

Elisa has created the very first set of multilingual online courses. For a list of available language combinations, visit her website: www.speakfromdayonewithelisa.com

Single-language courses are also available.

Language learning: common pitfalls and how to overcome them (coming soon)

Audiobooks and video courses will also be available soon.

Don't forget to subscribe to Elisa's YouTube channel: 'PassionForLanguages'.

Follow her on Instagram: speakfromdayonewithelisa

...a BIG thank you...

Publishing is harder than I thought and more rewarding than I could have ever imagined.

I'm eternally grateful to Nicolò who has always supported and helped me. Working together makes everything special and fun. Thank you!

A very special thanks to Ivan (SdruToons), who helped me transform my idea into the logo that I really like. I am also very grateful for all his precious support, and for all the jumps and climbing we did together.

A very special thanks to my editor, Emily, who helped and supported me. I really enjoy working with you!

To my wonderful twin sister Violetta, a source of love and inspiration. Thank you for all the laughter and moments we have shared.

A truthful thank you to my friend and coach Stephen. His positivity is inspiring and his friendship fulfilling.

I would also like to thank all my inspiring and supportive friends, my family and in particular my wonderful dad.

So thankful to have you all in my life!

Copyright

46067650R00065

Printed in Poland
by Amazon Fulfillment
Poland Sp. z o.o., Wrocław